William Porter

Alcohol Explained 2

For D.B.

## Table of Contents

1. Introduction ............................................................................. 5
2. The Key to Quitting ............................................................. 11
3. Addressing the Underlying Problems That Cause us to Drink ............................................................................................ 16
4. Alcohol and Sleep ............................................................... 31
5. Ambition ............................................................................. 41
6. Social Media and our Heroes and Heroines ...................... 49
7. Alcohol and Our Emotions ................................................ 57
8. You Made me Drink ........................................................... 62
9. Moderation .......................................................................... 71
10. Why do Humans Suffer From Addiction? ........................ 95
11. Stopping Drinking and Weightloss ................................. 107
12. Drinking Myths and Platitudes ....................................... 123
13. The Binge Drinker ............................................................ 147
14. The Tools for Quitting - When to Quit .......................... 152
15. The Tools for Quitting - Taking the Bull by the Horns .... 160
16. The Tools for Quitting - The Tipping Point ................... 164
17. The Tools for Quitting - Cravings .................................. 178

18. The Tools for Quitting - The Worst Drink You'll Ever Drink .................................................................................. 187
19. The Tools for Quitting - Self-Image ................................. 194
20. The Tools for Quitting - The Key Drinking Occasions ... 202
21. The Tools for Quitting - The Bad Days ........................... 215
22. The Tools for Quitting - Religion ..................................... 219
23. The Tools for Quitting – A Positive Approach ................. 222
24. Conclusion ........................................................................ 229

# 1. Introduction

One of the benefits of self-publishing a book on Amazon is that it is very easy to amend. Publishing a book is as simple as uploading a Word document and to amend the book you just amend the Word document and upload it again. So when Alcohol Explained was originally published I found myself updating it quite regularly. My ideas and my understanding of alcohol and addiction has been a journey and one that has continued since I originally published Alcohol Explained back in April 2015. So as my ideas and understanding progressed and developed, so did the book.

That was all well and good when the book existed only as an eBook and a paperback, but as Alcohol Explained became more and more popular I found I was getting more and more requests to produce an audio version. So I then produced the audio version. This had the effect of making the book a lot harder to amend; it is one thing to amend a word document and upload it, and quite another to have to engage the narrator to re-record sections of the book. This didn't unduly phase me however, I thought I would just stop amending and adding to it on such a regular basis. I would just wait until there was a significant amount of updating to do then I would do it and have the audio version re-recorded.

The problem was that when I finally got around to preparing for the rewrite there were two issues. Firstly, I found that the additional information that I wanted to include was almost as long as the original book. When I first wrote Alcohol Explained I tried to write the book that I wanted to read, not only in terms of content but also in terms of presentation. When I read self-help books I want them to be short and to the point. I want to get to the information as quickly as possible so I can implement it (or disregard it) and improve my life as soon as possible. I find very thick, text-heavy self-help books to be off-putting, and suffering from the aftereffects of drinking (which many of my readers are likely to be) will exacerbate this. This is also why I have spaced out the text in the paperback even though it increases the printing cost and cuts back on the royalties. I wanted the book to be concise and easy to read and doubling the length of it was going to defeat this goal entirely.

Secondly I had had the book translated into French. The translator was also a professional editor and during the translation process she approached me a few times about parts of the book that she thought were badly written, irrelevant, or detracted generally from it. Usually these were parts of the book that I was particularly pleased with and in one case was a part of the book that I felt was one of the strongest parts. I downloaded afresh the Kindle version because on Kindle there is an option to see what parts of a book people highlight regularly. I found a lot of parts had been highlighted that I would not have thought twice about rewriting or removing entirely. Alcohol Explained has proved a popular and helpful book. I didn't want to rewrite it and inadvertently make it less effective.

So for all these reasons I decided to write Alcohol Explained 2. It is essentially the natural progression of the ideas, concepts and general approach that formed the original Alcohol Explained. Some of it is developing ideas and concepts that were in the original, some of it is covering certain aspects in more detail, and some of it is introducing new concepts and tools. If anything it is more focussed towards quitting than the original Alcohol Explained.

The other thing I need to mention is the issue of scientific references. My lack of scientific references is the main (and almost sole) criticism of Alcohol Explained. There is much I could say on this subject but I will try to keep it brief. My understanding of alcohol and how it affects us and how it becomes addictive is, as far as I am aware, new. It is based to a small degree on existing science (essentially that alcohol is a chemical depressant and that the human brain seeks to maintain a balance). I haven't bothered to reference this because it seemed to me to not need referencing; it is widely known and if anyone does feel the need to go back to the sources they can do so using Google. Most of the rest of what I cover is my own observations and conclusions derived from my own experiences. I can't reference it because it is (as far as I am aware) new. My ideas have essentially been a process of starting with a few unarguable facts, and from there following them along to their logical conclusions using common sense and my own experiences. What I have tried to do is take the reader on the same journey I took, using common sense, logic and personal experience rather than scientific references. So when I describe the basic mechanism of alcohol being a chemical depressant, and the brain seeking to maintain a chemical balance, and then go on to describe how alcohol causes anxiety and disturbs sleep, for most people the three-pronged approach of a sound starting point, common sense and their own experiences of how well they sleep when they are drinking, and how they feel the next day, is enough to convince them that it is the truth. I can't help but feel that if that is not enough and that a scientific reference is also needed then I have very much missed my mark. For me, my approach is far more effective than just saying that alcohol causes sleep disturbance and anxiety, then quoting a scientific reference to back it up. Experience and common sense are, for me, far more powerful than quoting a scientific reference (which itself will be open to criticism and different interpretations) so this is the approach I have taken. It was never my intention to write a scientific treatise on the subject but to explain the entire phenomenon in the simple, layman's terms that I understand it in. With all of my books, I have taken the approach of writing a book that I myself would want to read and judging from the reception so far the vast majority of people are happy with this approach.

The final thing I would like to mention in this introduction is repetition within the book. The hardest thing I have found about writing on this topic is what order to cover off the various parts of it. It is possible to break down drinking into its various component parts and talk about them but they all interlink with one another and they all influence and often exacerbate one another. If you want to cover a topic fully you have to link it with other topics in order to contextualise it and also to tie it in with other elements that may increase its influence. This means I am constantly having to refer to some topics several times as I tie them in with new topics. This causes some necessary degree of repetition. If this irritates you I apologise in advance and hope you will bear with me. I have done the best I can in the circumstances.

With that said, now let's move on to the book itself. One of the first things that I think is useful to cover is why Alcohol Explained is so useful for quitting drinking. After all something in the region of 80% of the book is taken up with explaining the whole alcohol and addiction phenomenon, and the parts providing tools on quitting are the 20% tagged on at the end. Yes we know the platitudes that 'knowledge is power' and 'know your enemy' but why is a full and complete understanding of the alcohol trap the key to successfully quitting for so many people?

## 2. The Key to Quitting

The key to quitting alcohol or any drug is to materially change how we perceive that drug. Addiction, any addiction, comes about because a part of the addict believes that they need the drug to fully enjoy or cope with life. Yes there is the physical side to drugs, that horrible withdrawal period that leaves us feeling miserable or anxious or scared, but the physical side is not the addiction. If it were, then any one of the many drugs that remove or lessen with withdrawal would provide the key to freedom and once through the physical withdrawal phase every addict would be free for life.

The drug may be dragging the addict down, killing them and ruining their life but while they believe that they cannot enjoy life or cope with life without it they will continue to return to it. Every time they feel low, every time something bad happens to them, every time they are in a group and don't feel part of it, every time they feel like their life has no meaning, they will be dragged back. It is this belief, that they truly need the drug, that is the very essence of addiction. This is why telling people that it is them and not the drug that is the problem is so damaging. It is not only incorrect but it instils into them the belief that they are incomplete without their drug and that there is a genuine reason for them to keep taking it.

This makes alcohol by far the hardest drug to quit because it is alcohol over and above any other drug in the Western world where we face daily from the vast majority of the population the repeated message that we need it to enjoy life. Don't believe me? How many times have you refused a drink at a social function and had someone try to talk you into having one? Never mind that you are driving, take a cab! Never mind that you are on a health kick, start again another day! And why is there so much pressure to drink? Because at social occasions our hosts and hostesses want us to enjoy ourselves and they and everyone else 'knows' you cannot enjoy yourself fully without a drink. Think of the platitudes that are so well known that we don't even bother to question them anymore. 'A night out is more fun when you have a few drinks!' But what does this actually mean? It means a night out is less fun if you aren't drinking, which in turn means that if you don't drink on a night out you won't enjoy yourself properly. Which itself in turn means that you need a chemical substance to fully enjoy your life.

Every time you put on your TV there is a film or TV show depicting people drinking to relax, to have fun, to deal with stress, to bond. Turn off your TV and you see it everywhere, with friends, acquaintances, and colleagues. The only drug that ever came close to this was nicotine but in recent years smoking has been frowned upon more and more so now it is alcohol that stands head and shoulders above any other drug where we are continually bombarded with messages that we need it to enjoy and cope with our lives. This makes it incredibly difficult to quit.

Fortunately for those of us who wish to quit we have the truth on our side. When you understand drinking fully you not only appreciate that alcohol drags you down far more than you originally believed, but crucially you also start to understand that the vast majority of the assumed benefits of drinking are an illusion. This is why a full understanding is key. We drink for the supposed benefits and once you understand that those benefits are false and illusionary you can lose the desire to drink at all. This is the real reason why understanding is such a powerful tool in quitting; it is because alcohol doesn't provide a tenth of the benefits we actually think it does and it has far more negative consequences in terms of quality of life than most people realise. Think of addiction like a set of scales in your mind. On the one side of the scales are all the reasons you drink and on the other side all the reasons you should stop. A full understanding removes a huge amount from the 'keep drinking' side of the scales and adds a huge amount to the 'stop drinking' side of the scales. Pretty soon you end up with a set of scales with several tons on the 'stop' side and a few ounces on the 'carry on' side and when you get to this stage your problem is effectively solved.

If alcohol genuinely provided even half of what we ascribe to it then these books would be a waste of time, there would just be chapter after chapter about how good alcohol makes you feel and how hard life is without it. Fortunately this is not the case. Alcohol is its own worst enemy. It takes much and gives little (if anything). The real problem is that we humans have created a whole smoke screen around it and perpetrate the illusion that it has numerous benefits; that it's fun and enjoyable and sociable. A simple exercise of deduction and common sense and the application of a little knowledge, understanding and perception can blow all of this away leaving us seeing alcohol as it really is; a rather pathetic little chemical that has some use as a disinfectant and running motor vehicles and little else. We also stop envying the so called 'normal drinkers' and start to look on them with pity. We see them as they really are; human beings who have been tricked into taking an unpleasant little drug that takes so much and gives so little. They may be at an earlier stage in their addiction to us (although more often than not the reality is that that they are just at a different stage in the denial of their addcition than us). Once we see alcohol in this light, as it really is, and stop seeing it as a magical elixir that can solve all our problems in the tip of a wrist, our problem is effectively at an end.

One of the reasons that we find it so hard to accept that alcohol gives so little is because time and again we proved to ourselves through personal experience that when the going gets tough, a drink takes the edge off things. In fact this is now so deeply ingrained in our thinking that addiction professionals will often recommend to a client that they need to address the underlying problems that they have that lead to them drinking before they even make the attempt to quit. In the next Chapter we will analyse this aspect in detail.

## 3. Addressing the Underlying Problems That Cause us to Drink

As we know alcohol is a chemical depressant and when you drink your brain takes various steps to counter the depressive effects of the alcohol. When the alcohol then wears off you are left feeling overly anxious and nervous. This is covered in detail right at the start of Alcohol Explained but it is such a key point that I think it is worth running through it again here, not least because since originally publishing Alcohol Explained I've been lucky enough to have been asked to give several talks on this subject and I have found that the use of slides to illustrate the concept can be very effective. These slides are of course a vast oversimplification of the complicated and intricate chemical and physiological processes at play but it is how I (and many others) understand it.

Firstly it helps to broadly categorise all the chemicals, drugs and hormones that the brain creates and excretes into two main categories; stimulants and depressants. Stimulants are things that wake us up, make us feel more alert and increase our heart rate. Our brain secretes these when we need to wake up or when it senses a threat or when we start a physical activity. Depressants on the other hand are those things that decrease or inhibit nerve activity. They make us feel relaxed and calm and our brain releases them when it is time to rest or sleep.

Of course it's not as simple as your brain just squirting out chemicals, it is far more complicated than that. It's not just the release of the chemical but also for example how long that chemical remains in your system for and how sensitive the reactors in your brain that respond to it are. However in terms of a simple understanding of how it works, it is useful to think of a weighing scale or a graph showing the stimulant and the depressant balance at work.

So this first graph is our natural, alcohol free, state. As you can see the stimulants and depressants are roughly equal. This balance means we are feeling good mentally; confident, resilient, and generally quite happy.

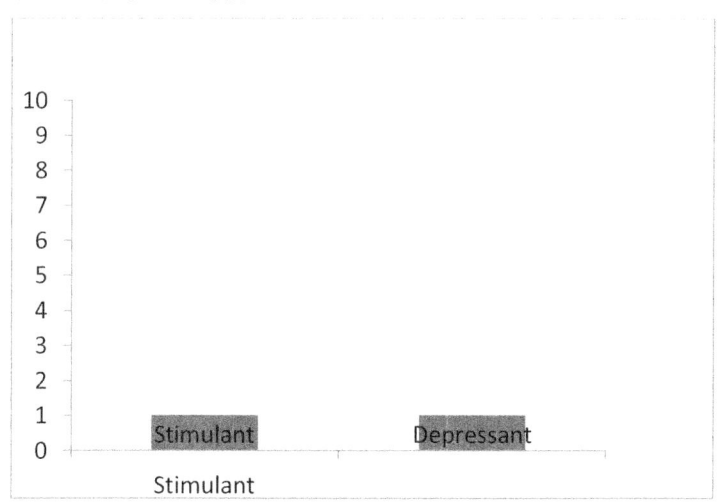

[Bar graph showing Stimulant and Depressant at roughly equal low levels, y-axis 0-10]

We then drink. The results of this are shown in this second graph. As you can see the alcohol has a depressing effect (and when I use the word 'depressing' I am using it in its chemical sense, as something that depresses or inhibits nerve activity), leaving us mentally dulled and uncoordinated.

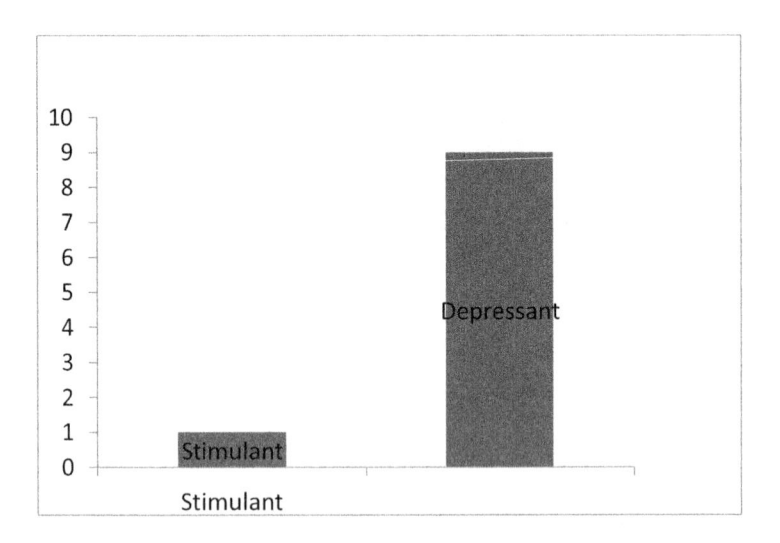

The brain looks to counter this sudden upset to the delicate chemical balance that it is constantly seeking to maintain. As mentioned previously the mechanics of this are complicated but for the purposes of understanding how alcohol affects us the mechanism is less important than the effect which is that the brain counters the depressant effects of the alcohol by increasing the stimulant side of the scales.

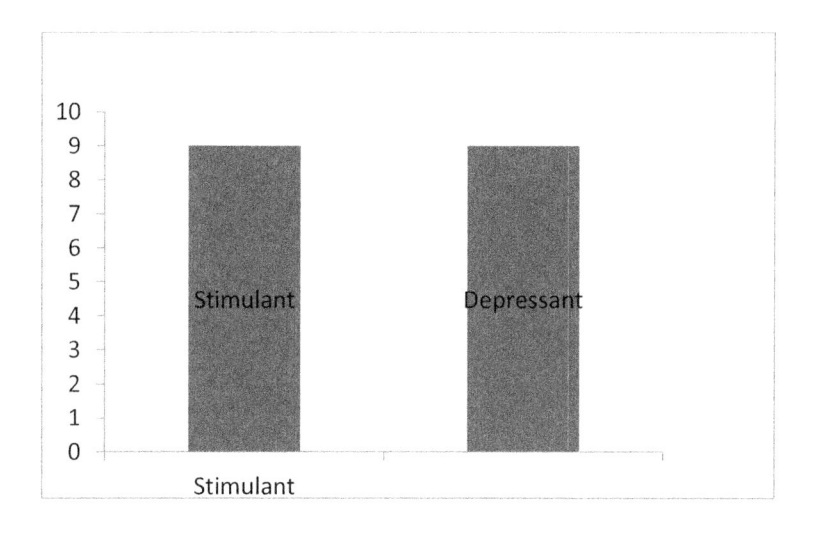

[Bar chart showing Stimulant and Depressant both at 9]

The alcohol then wears off with the effect that the brain is then overly stimulated and there is now a chemical imbalance. This is shown in the next graph and is essentially the alcohol withdrawal phase. This is the phase when we are anxious, nervous, and generally feel out of sorts and less able to cope with things. It is caused by a chemical imbalance that is itself a direct cause of the alcohol we have consumed.

[Bar chart: Stimulant = 9, Depressant = 1]

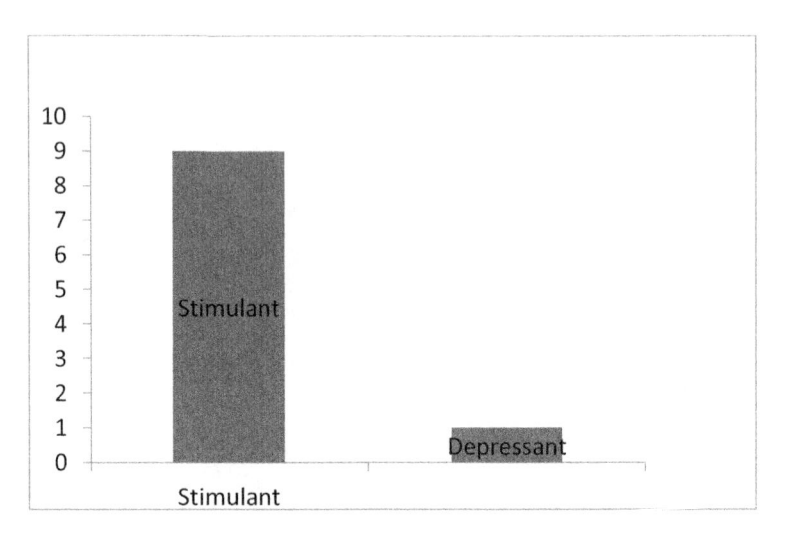

The quickest way to rectify this imbalance is to take another dose of alcohol which counters the excess stimulant level and redresses the chemical imbalance caused by the previous intake of alcohol.

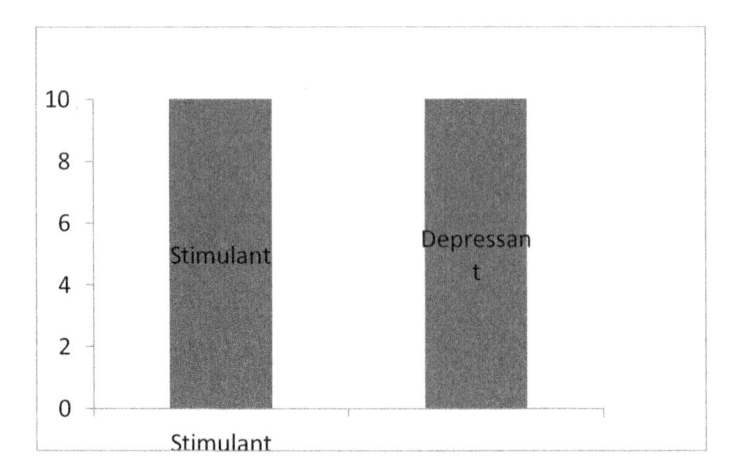

[Bar chart: Stimulant = 10, Depressant = 10]

20

These last two graphs represent the world in which regular drinkers live. Their daily drinks relieve that horrible anxious, out of sorts feeling leave them feeling courageous, happy, and able to cope with life. It is a wonderful feeling but it is a feeling that essentially comes from having a good natural balance in our brains. It is the feeling they would have all the time had they not interfered with the chemical balance in their brains in the first place.

It can take several days after your last drink for this feeling of fear to dissipate, but a far quicker way to get rid of it is to drink more. After all, the fear is caused by hypersensitivity that your brain has triggered so that it can work under the depressive effects of the alcohol. More alcohol counters that fear so you go back to feeling normal. This is the main benefit of drinking for regular drinkers; it removes fear and anxiety caused by the previous drinking. Of course the withdrawal isn't the only aspect of this. Drinking also disturbs our sleep with the effect that regular drinkers are always more tired and drained than they would otherwise be. This again has a knock-on effect on our peace of mind and confidence; if you are tired you feel less able to cope generally and less buoyant and positive. In the next Chapter we will look at sleep in more detail but for now let's stick with the withdrawal and our problems.

Because it takes a few days to fully recover from the post drinking fear, regular drinkers never fully recover from it, they just yo-yo between post-drinking induced fear and relieving that drinking induced fear by drinking more. All the regular drinker knows of life is that life when not drinking is a life of fear, anxiety, timidity, and an inability to cope. Life when drinking is a life of confidence, boldness, spirit and fortitude. It may not be as extreme as this; the more you drink the worse the post drinking anxiety, but even one glass of wine a night will have this effect, albeit less pronounced than the bottle of spirits a day drinker.

A lot of people grasp this concept quite quickly on an academic level but then fail to link it on a practical level to their own drinking. In the years since Alcohol Explained was first published I have come into contact with a lot of people who have stopped drinking for many months or years then started again and found themselves becoming crippled with anxiety, depression, or their past experiences. I am often asked if I think they should go on medication or seek counselling before trying to quit because (they say) alcohol is their only relief from this misery. I find myself time and again explaining that drinking doesn't relieve anxiety and depression, it causes it. And the deciding point? That invariably the anxiety and depression wasn't apparent (or at least was substantially reduced) during their period of sobriety.

Even drinkers who do not drink regularly suffer from the withdrawal. Essentially any feeling of comfort, confidence or relaxation you obtain from drinking then has a corresponding feeling of anxiety. This is a feeling of being nervous and afraid, molehills start to look like mountains. It is in essence a feeling of being unable to cope with problems. It is doubt, worry, fear and timidity. The more you drink, the more extreme this post drinking fear becomes.

Everyone faces problems in their life. Some big. Some small. Some in between. We tend to have more of the smaller ones and less of the larger ones. Smaller ones might be paying a bill, querying a charge on a credit card bill, completing a tax return. The larger ones might be relationship problems, redundancy, financial problems, serious illness, the loss of a loved one. The smaller ones are almost just irritants, annoying little things that have to be dealt with. The larger ones are more overpowering, and by overpowering I mean they can require more energy to deal with, sometimes more energy than we feel we can muster. They tend to be things that often we feel we can do nothing about.

So we have these problems, ranging from minor to very serious. Let's give them a scale of 1 – 10 just for the purposes of illustration, with 1 being the least serious and 10 being the most serious.

Let's also assume that a normal mentally and physically healthy person will be able to deal with all the problems up to, say, 8 or 9, and will be unable to cope with only the most serious of problems (which we hope are relatively few and far between).

What the alcohol withdrawal actually does is to prevent us from being able to cope or deal with problems we would otherwise tackle with little or no consternation. The very serious withdrawal of the late stage alcoholic will leave them unable to cope with any problem, right down to severity 1. A more medium withdrawal will leave you unable to cope with, say, any problem exceeding a 7. All this is arbitrary and for illustrative purposes only but hopefully you are getting the idea.

This was certainly the case for me. When I was drinking I would go into work at the beginning of the week on a Monday or Tuesday (or even a Wednesday after a particularly bad weekend) and I would be incapable of doing anything but the most basic of tasks. For the vast majority of things I had to do I would be like a rabbit caught in the headlights of a car. I was absolutely frozen, I just didn't feel able to deal with them. However after a day or two when the withdrawal had worn off I would be dealing with these tasks without batting an eyelid. I used to do 5 days work in three most weeks.

This is why the withdrawal is so powerful; it leaves us feeling unable to cope with life. It is a horrible feeling. But if you then take a drink you negate the withdrawal and again feel like you can deal with all but the most serious of problems. And that is why people will put the drink before family, friends, work, even their very lives. I think it is also worth mentioning here that what alcohol does is make you feel like you COULD deal with your problems, however when you are actually drinking you rarely do actually deal with any of them. It essentially just anaesthetises them. You tend to go through alternating states of being so worried by your problems that you feel unable to deal with them, to being ambivalent towards them, but you scarcely ever actually do anything about them with the result that they tend to accumulate and become even more overpowering; after all even the 1s, 2s and 3s can be overpowering if we are overwhelmed by the sheer number of them. Also the 1s and 2s (like paying a bill) will quickly turn into 4s or 5s if we ignore them for long enough.

The tendency is for drinkers to be either actually drinking in which case they have no interest whatsoever in dealing with any of their problems as the drink has negated their fear of them and hence negated their desire to do anything about them. Alternatively they are hungover and / or in the withdrawal period in which case they simply don't feel mentally able to deal with them.

This is why some people are more prone to gravitate towards problem drinking than others. Those who don't gravitate towards problem drinking tend to be people who are comfortable in their career in that they can do their job standing on their head, it presents them no real challenges (either because it is not challenging or because they have been doing it for so long that there is nothing new for them). They also tend to be fairly happy in both their family and financial situation. They simply don't have any serious problems to deal with day to day.

Whatever your problem is, no matter how terrible and overpowering, post drinking anxiety will make it worse and if you are drinking regularly then the only time you aren't going through the post drinking anxiety is when you are drinking again. So the only time your problem looks even slightly manageable is when you are drinking. So you are fooled into thinking that alcohol is helping when it isn't.

If you have a genuine problem then the first thing you need to do is to assess it to decide what you need to do about it. Imagine you are the Commander-in-Chief of a military force. You receive reports of a threat. The first thing you need to do is fully and accurately assess what that threat is. Is it irrelevant and so can be totally disregarded? Is it real but small, so that a few aggressive patrols might see it off? Or is it a full-scale military force on a footing with your own, such that full mobilisation and total offensive is required? How can you make a decision if half the reports you receive say the threat is just a toddler with a water pistol, and the other half say it's a military force 20 times more powerful than your own?

This is why, when people are drinking a lot and they go to their doctor with symptoms of depression or anxiety, often the doctor won't prescribe anything but will tell them first to quit drinking. At least this is what the doctor should do if they are both responsible and properly aware of the effects of regular consumption of alcohol. Some people do have chemical imbalances in their brain which they are born with (i.e. are not created by outside chemical interference). These people may need medication to address this, but human understanding of the human brain is at its infancy and we do not have a complete list of all the chemicals, drugs and hormones that the brain creates and excretes, let alone do we understand the delicate chemical balance between them. There is currently a body of opinion that says that mental health issues are not the result of chemical imbalances but have other causes. Whatever the actual position is, taking drugs to deal with mental health issues is, at this stage in our medical understanding, largely guesswork and requires very close collaboration between the medical professional and the patient, so that the exact effects of any particular medication can be continually assessed, in particular to see what side effects there are and so that constant tweaking and readjustments can be made. This delicate process is virtually impossible when the brain is in constant turmoil from the constant swinging between over depressant / over simulation that is caused by regular drinking.

So the first problem with saying that you need to address your underlying problems before you quit drinking is that you cannot effectively address a problem, any problem, when suffering from post-drinking induced fear. Nor can you effectively address a problem when you're drinking.

Secondly whatever problems you deal with new ones pop up to take their place. I don't care who you are or what you have in life, everyone has their problems. Even if you could deal with every single one of your problems every day, new ones would come along to take their place. Stopping drinking isn't about first remedying all your underlying problems, it is about learning to deal with, and coping with, all the slings and arrows of outrageous fortune without recourse to alcohol. If your sobriety relies on you not having any problems to deal with then you've already failed.

The fact of the matter is, whatever problem you are suffering from, it never looks so bad as when you are in the middle of post drinking anxiety. The peace and confidence that comes from long term sobriety is precisely what you need to give you the best chance to start tackling those problems that we all suffer from to a greater or lesser degree.

Alcohol is a drug that erodes our confidence and our ability to deal with day to day life. It then partially restores that ability, thus creating the illusion of being a necessary and crucial part of our lives. It is alcohol that often makes our problems appear insurmountable, and a period of sobriety is often what we need to rediscover the inner strength required to actually properly deal with those issues.

Saying that you need to deal with your underlying issues before you stop drinking is like saying you need to run a marathon then do the training for it. If you need to tackle a challenge, you need to be in your best form to do it. For a physical challenge you need to be at your best physically, for a mental or emotional challenge you need to be at your best mentally and emotionally. You cannot be in this best mental and emotional condition unless you first stop drinking and put an end to the endless rounds of chemically induced highs and consequential lows.

If you have managed to live with a problem when its effect on you is being constantly warped by the emotional yo-yoing caused by drinking, then you are going to be able to survive it when you have the confidence and emotional stability you get from long term sobriety. Stopping drinking will turn mountains back into molehills and those few genuine mountains can start to appear less insurmountable. If you stop drinking and discover that you genuinely suffer from anxiety or depression or any other mental health issue then you have just taken the first step in being able to properly address it and deal with it.

I once sat in an AA meeting and listened to a lady who was in a car with her husband and two children. They were in a crash and although she managed to get out her husband and two children were trapped inside. The fuel tank caught alight and she watched them burn to death, trying in vain again and again to get them out and getting horrifically burned herself in the process. She had not only managed to stop drinking but had also managed to find some degree of peace and hope. How she managed to do that is utterly beyond me, but it demonstrates the ability of human beings to deal with the most horrific things if only we give ourselves the opportunity to, instead of just seeking chemically induced anaesthesia and exacerbating the effects that incident has on us.

As mentioned previously it isn't just the alcohol induced chemical imbalance of the brain that erodes our self-confidence, mental resilience and peace of mind, it is also the lack of good quality sleep. I briefly looked at how alcohol affects sleep in Alcohol Explained but let's now delve into this topic in more detail.

# 4. Alcohol and Sleep

When we are looking at how alcohol affects sleep we need to understand three things; how our brain works, how alcohol affects it and sleep.

The first two parts have been dealt with in the preceding Chapter so now let's now consider sleep.

As with our understanding of the human brain, our understanding of 'sleep' is in its infancy. There is much that we as human beings do not understand about sleep, but again fortunately to understand how alcohol affects sleep we only need to understand the basics which are this; we sleep in different cycles and one of the main differentiating factors of these cycles is how deeply asleep we are. One of the cycles of sleep is REM (Rapid Eye Movement) sleep. REM sleep is categorised by rapid movement of the eyes, increased heart rate and parts of the brain show activity similar to if you were awake. It is closely associated with dreaming. Essentially it is a period of sleep in which you are raised up from deep sleep into a state that is very close to being awake. No one actually knows what the purpose of REM sleep is, but what we do know is that it is essential. In tests, rats that have been deprived of REM sleep die within 4 to 6 weeks.

So now we've got the basics in place; how our brains work, how alcohol affects us, and sleep. So what happens when we put them all together?

When you drink and then go to sleep the depressant effects of the alcohol holds sway. You can't get into REM sleep because that arena of sleep requires you to be very close to waking; your brain needs to raise you up to just below the level of full consciousness. Being drugged on alcohol your brain struggles to raise you to this level, so for the first 4 or 5 hours your brain finds it extremely difficult to put you into the REM sleep cycle. You either have no REM sleep, or far less (and far worse quality) than you ought to have.

After this 4 or 5 hour period the alcohol has usually worn off to such an extent that the residual stimulants now outweigh the depressants and the effect of this is that it is generally impossible to get to sleep at all. This is why so many people find that after drinking they wake in the middle of the night completely unable to get back to sleep. Even if they do manage to sleep it is usually fitful and spasmodic. They can be absolutely exhausted, their bodies crying out for sleep, but they will be unable to sleep because the effect of the residual simulants leaves them totally unable to sleep. It's like trying to sleep after 8 or 9 mugs of very strong coffee.

Imagine you need 8 hours sleep a night to be at your best. Imagine if you decided to set an alarm to wake yourself up after 4 hours and when this alarm went off you got up and drank 8 mugs of strong black coffee and then lay there, tossing and turning and fidgeting and twitching for all the rest of the night. This is exactly what you do when you drink alcohol. Imagine doing that night after night, for days and weeks and months and years. Imagine what it would do to you, imagine the effect on your physical and mental health. Sleep deprivation is used as torture, and it is a highly effective one. There is a lot that we as human beings don't know about sleep but what is abundantly clear is that sleep is when your body and brain repairs itself and recuperates. Have you ever been mulling over a problem then woken up one day and just known what to do about it? When you sleep your body continues to digest food, to break it down into manageable pieces so it can be properly dealt with. Your mind does exactly the same with all the information and experiences that it absorbs during the day. Sleep is key to our mental and physical wellbeing. Alcohol robs us of that.

This is why, after drinking, you can be in bed for 8, 10 or 12 hours and still end up starting the day tired and drained. It is also worth bearing in mind that even just one or two drinks is enough to upset the delicate chemical balance of the brain and will lead to disturbed sleep.

For many people, myself included, getting decent quality sleep and waking up refreshed and raring to go is one of the great benefits of not drinking. It makes the entire exercise of giving up drinking worthwhile on its own, to say nothing of all the other related benefits. For this reason it can be very frustrating for people who give up alcohol but still find they are still sleeping badly. There are a few things to say on this topic.

Firstly of course you do not give up drinking on day one, and wake up on day 2 feeling refreshed and ready to face the world. It does take a small amount of time to get back into a normal sleeping pattern after you give up drinking. In fact there are four stages that you need to go through before you wake up feeling well rested and ready to face the day:

1. The Alcohol.
The first and most obvious one is the alcohol needs to leave your system. On average it takes one hour for your liver to process one unit of alcohol (one unit being 25ml / 0.85oz of spirits, 76ml / 2.5oz of wine, or 250ml / 8.5oz of beer). So if you've drunk 3 bottles of spirits it could take around three and a half days for that alcohol to be processed. Most people probably won't be drinking to that level, but many people don't really keep track of what they drink. A good rule of thumb is that the average person will need about 24 hours to rid themselves of all the alcohol.

2. Excess Stimulants.

For most drinkers their problems really start to kick in after the alcohol has left their system because this is when the stimulants are in full sway. One of the key parts of how our brain reacts to the depressive effects of the alcohol is that over time the human brain become more effective at countering the alcohol and one of the ways in which it does this is to create and secrete more and more of the stimulants it uses to counter the ever increasing amounts of alcohol that we drink (this is how we can drink more and more as the years go by). How long these stimulants will take to leave your body will depend on both the individual (long term heavier drinkers will have more of these than lighter drinkers) and the amount drunk in the previous session. For this reason it is not possible to put a firm time frame on it but the majority of people will be through this stage within 24 hours, the worst case being around 72 hours (so 1 to 3 days).

3. The Final Balancing.
The above 2 stages will be the end of the process for intermittent, binge drinkers. However for people who drink regularly (i.e. every day or most days) there is a final stage to go through. As you can see from the graphs in the previous chapter (and in particular the final two), those who drink every day are simply yo-yoing between the 'excess stimulant' phase and the drinking phase. They never actually rid themselves of the stimulants (they are drinking and causing the brain to secrete more stimulants before the last lot has been

processed). So after 2 to six days of not drinking, the stimulants are finally processed and are not replaced. Because the individual will have become used to having these excess stimulants inside of them for virtually all the time, and because these excess stimulants are now gone, they will feel very tired and lethargic. It is much the same process as if they were drinking 8 or 9 cups of strong coffee every day and suddenly cut it out. This is a period of tiredness, lethargy and feeling like you just want to sleep all the time and have no energy to do anything. It can take anything from 5 days to 3 weeks for the brain to acclimatise to this.

4. Sleep.
Whether you are going through the first two phases only or all three of them there is one final stage you also need to go through before you go back to feeling positive and confident again. This is to get a good night's sleep. We acclimatise to a sleeping pattern. If you set an alarm for 2am for a few nights, and get up at that time and go to toilet and maybe get a drink of water then you will get used to waking up at this time all the time. Equally if you have spent years waking up at 4 am every night, it will take you time to get back into a normal sleeping pattern. And of course when you do get back into a normal sleeping pattern you will need to get a few night's sleep to start to feel normal again. If you haven't had a decent night's sleep for years you won't catch up on the missed sleep after just one night.

To a large degree there is not much you can do to hurry the process of getting back to a normal sleeping pattern and waking up feeling refreshed and ready to go. Sleeping tablets for example tend to further interrupt your sleeping pattern and most people find it best to simply wait for their body and brain to find its own natural equilibrium. However there are a few things you can do to assist this natural process as far as possible. I list these below:

1. Try to cut down on caffeinated drinks, particularly later in the day. Definitely avoid caffeine in the evenings and, if you can, in the afternoon as well. Bear in mind also that nicotine is also a powerful stimulant and should be avoided as much as possible.

2. Try to do as much exercise / physical activity as you can, and as early in the day as you can manage. The more physical activity you have undertaken during the day the better you will sleep, but vigorous physical activity will increase oxygen flow and adrenaline which makes you feel more awake. So do as much as you can as early as you can.

3. Eating a large meal can make you feel tired as the body diverts significant resources to digestion, but the digestive process involves much internal movement and can generate a lot of heat. This can disturb your sleep. So try to have your main meal at lunchtime, and eat as light as you can in the evening. If you can manage it don't eat

at all after lunch. It may feel strange to begin with but the effect on quality of sleep is dramatic, particularly for those used to eating a lot in the evening.

4. If you are waking up regularly in the night you may be going to bed too early. If you need 8 hours sleep, and you are in bed for 9, then you are going to spend an hour of your time in bed awake, this usually ends up being in the middle of the night. If your routine allows it try to get up at the same time every day (even weekends / non workdays) as this gets you used to waking up at the same time. If you are then waking up in the night a lot you can then put your bedtime back a bit to find the right level. Having said this, if you are not feeling tired during the day then waking up at night isn't really anything to be too concerned about. If you are not drinking then waking up during the night tends to be a peaceful time. It is only when you are suffering from the post drinking anxiety that waking up in the night is such torture, as you lie there exhausted but unable to sleep, worrying about anything and everything.

5. No matter how tired you are, or how stringently you follow all these instructions, if you go to bed with your head full of things that worry or upset or anger you, you will struggle to sleep. One of the knacks to falling asleep is to get everything negative and upsetting out of your mind and to focus on something comforting and relaxing. As I say this is a knack, it takes time and effort but the more you do it the

easier it gets. Meditating is one way of doing this, or losing yourself in a good book, but essentially what it amounts to is filling your mind up with comforting, happy thoughts. You could focus on a particular thing that makes you happy, or indulge in a little night-time fantasy you create for yourself like hiding away somewhere safe and quiet and warm, but the key is to empty your mind of all the worries, stresses and strains of the day.

Having your brain return to its normal balanced state and waking up fully refreshed after a good night's sleep is one of the great pleasures of quitting alcohol. In fact one of the worst aspects of drinking is that people make so many sacrifices for it. They sacrifice money, slimness, fitness, sleep, life span, peace of mind, confidence, and resilience. And what do they get in return for all this that they sacrifice on the altar of alcohol? They get to anaesthetise, for a precious few hours every day, all the anxiety and exhaustion that's been caused by the previous drinking, and to return for a few moments to the feeling of peace and confidence that they would have all the time if they just quit for good. I am not saying that life is perfect when you stop drinking. Everyone, drinkers and non-drinkers alike, have good days and bad but the non-drinkers have the mental resilience and confidence to deal with their problems and still enjoy life.

So if life is so much better when you aren't regularly poisoning yourself with alcohol, why do so many people return to it after quitting? One aspect of this we have touched on already in this book; that we are constantly being bombarded with messages (some subtle, some more overt) that human beings need alcohol to fully enjoy and cope with life. Another aspect of this is Fading Effect Bias that I dealt with in Alcohol Explained. However since publishing Alcohol Explained another element of this has occurred to me. It is one of the basic driving forces of all living things, the drive to improve your lot in life. This driving force is also known as 'ambition'.

# 5. Ambition

When I talk about ambition I am talking about something far more than a simple desire to take the next step up whatever career ladder we've found ourselves trying to climb. I am talking about a very basic motivating factor in all living creatures; the desire to improve one's life. Ambition is a feeling within us, like a hunger, to always be moving on to the next challenge or the next improvement, to always be on the lookout for ways to improve or better ourselves. Some people will say that it is a personality trait of the so-called alcoholic to never be satisfied, to reach for one thing and as soon as they grasp it, to find fault with it and to then reach for the next thing. This isn't a personality trait of the so-called alcoholic, it is a personality trait of every healthy living creature.

Whether you believe we were created by a supreme being or are a process of natural selection, or a mixture of the two, the fact is that the species that are driven to improve their lives and the lives of their families are the species that are most likely to survive and thrive. If you are a hunter gatherer, living on stony soil with very little to hunt or gather, and you see a few miles distant a land of milk and honey, you have to have that driving force to force you to move to that other land.

Ambition isn't just about wanting something better, it is far more intricate than that. It is made up of two separate tendencies; the tendencies to look for fault in what we already have and to glorify and idealise what we don't have. It is these two tendencies together that make up the phenomenon that we think of as 'ambition'. It is a normal, natural motivating force for all living creatures and promotes improvement for the individual, the family and the species. We are always overly critical of what we do have and always tend to idolise what we don't have.

In fact this phenomenon can be seen in all aspects of human life. How many times have you wanted that perfect job, got it, been ecstatic, then been looking for the next job within a year or two? Or moved heaven and earth to move to a new house, been so happy to move, then found yourself looking at something bigger and better? How many times have you fought to get that perfect partner then found you can't get away from them quick enough? Or on the other side, how many times have you chased after someone again and again only to be rejected then given up on them, only for them to then show an interest? They don't want you while you're available, and only when you become unavailable do they suddenly want you. Ever looked at the billionaire and wondered why they were still working and trying to make even more money? They are as susceptible to this tendency as any of us.

Familiarity breeds contempt, the temptation of the forbidden fruit, the end of the honeymoon period. All these common phrases essentially describe the same process; that natural tendency to pick holes in what we do have and glorify what we don't have. This is the key concept; if something falls into the 'I have it' category then we view it harshly, we criticise it and look to find fault with it. If something falls into the 'I don't have it' category then we glorify it, idolise it, and desire it. We see only the good in it and we ignore or brush off the bad.

This is a natural and healthy tendency. It drives us to improve. The problem is the way in which this tendency interacts with drugs and contributes to addiction.

While we're drinking our drinking falls into the 'I have it' category. We tend towards finding fault with it and, frankly, that is all too easy to do. The insomnia, the exhaustion, the anxiety, the blackouts, the arguments, the cost in terms of finances and strain it puts on our personal relationships, and all for the dubious 'pleasure' of drinking a sticky poisonous mess that dulls, for a few brief moments, all the exhaustion and anxiety it caused in the first place. Well there's an obvious solution to that problem, the solution is staring us in the face; quit! So we make an attempt to quit. We have a few days of physical withdrawal and after that we start feeling better than we ever did when we were drinking. We've done what we once thought we could never do, we are free and we are loving it!

The problem is that having now quit, alcohol has now moved from the 'I have it' category, into the 'I don't have it' category. So we stop thinking of it critically and start idolising it. The insomnia, the exhaustion, the anxiety, the blackouts, the arguments, and all the downside of our drinking are forgotten. Now we are thinking only of those drinks we really enjoyed. We see ourselves sitting out on a sun deck on holiday with a cold drink in our hands, we see ourselves at Christmas with friends and family enjoying a nice glass of mulled wine, we see ourselves in a cosy pub with our good friends, laughing and enjoying life. If you analyse this sensibly you'll realise how nonsensical this thinking is. How many drinks have you drunk over the course of your life? How many fall into that category of really enjoyable? How many drinks did you have on a sun deck on holiday, compared with sitting at home in front of the TV on another depressing night in? Those truly enjoyable drinks are few and far between but it is these that we think about even though they are completely unrepresentative of the reality of drinking.

So we forget the bad and we think only of the good. We don't think about the hangovers, the arguments, the blackouts, the anxiety, the exhaustion, the self-loathing, the waking up at night exhausted but also unable to sleep, the lying there awake worrying about anything and everything, the impact on our relationships, on our finances, on our friendships. In essence we forget that we hated it and desperately wanted to stop. We idolise, we fantasise, we build up in our minds a utopia of drinking that never existed to begin with.

It's little surprise that given this tendency so many people end up drinking again. After all if drinking was what we imagine it to be when we are idolising it we'd never have stopped to begin with. In fact no one would ever stop!

The other issue of course is that we forget what it was like to be controlled by a chemical, to be under its power. In essence we forget what it is to be addicted. When we stop we soon return to our optimum mental resilience and with our new found mental resilience we would find quitting anything far easier. We feel confident and resilient and in control, and in the same way we can't imagine why we drank for so long so we also can't properly remember why we found it so hard to stop. We lose our fear of becoming addicted again.

This is why addicts so often return to their drugs even when they are well past the physical withdrawal phase. It's particularly the case with drinking because we are constantly bombarded with the false images of alcohol being a fun, harmless and healthy thing, more so than any other drug out there.

So we lose our fear of addiction, we idolise drinking, we are constantly bombarded with all the lies and nonsense that make people drink in the first place, and unless we are guarding against all of these things we end up drinking again.

The problem is that when we start drinking again we return to the reality of drinking and not the idolised fantasy. What we return to is not the paradise we've been pining for but the living hell we wanted to escape from in the first place. The fantasy evaporates and reality comes crashing back in. Our drinking moves from the 'I don't have it' into the 'I have it' category. All this may happen while drinking that first drink or it may take a few hours or even a few days but it will happen. Pretty soon we are back to where we started which is doing something we hate and desperately looking for a way to quit. And so the process continues.

This is the central frustration of the addict; what they miss and keep returning to never existed to begin with. It is pure fantasy that exists only in their mind. It is essentially the shift in perception between how we see something that we have, and how we see something that we have given up. Ambition is one of the reasons many addicts are constantly moving between taking the drug and abstaining. They are miserable when they are taking the drug but because stopping means giving up something they believe they enjoy, they are miserable when they stop. So they are constantly looking to make a change between imbibing and abstaining. The problem is of course there is no third way; they either take the drug or they don't. They are miserable either way so they are constantly flitting between the two. Sure, they can try to moderate, but with drugs the natural tendency is to take more and more so eventually the intake slides back to where it was and they want to stop again.

This is a key point to keep at the front of your mind. When you quit, if you ever start thinking that a drink might be nice then remember that it is the idea and not the reality of that drink that is drawing you in. It's like a trap that is sprung by using a hologram, something ethereal that does not exist. Trust me, if drinking is how you imagine it after you quit, I for one would still be drinking!

There are no great steps you need to take to counter this you just need to be aware of it and to expect it. Expect that after you've successfully quit there will come a time when the idea of a drink seems attractive. Just anticipate this and understand that it is false. This is why assisting others to escape the alcohol trap can be beneficial for the helper as well as those being helped. It keeps in mind the truth about what those drinking years were really like. For those who don't have time to actively go out and assist others the Alcohol Explained Facebook Group is a good option. It allows you to provide help and assistance on an ad hoc basis, and also keeps you in contact with people at all stages of their sober journey including those who seem to be endlessly repeating day one and those who have relapsed. Reading their posts is a stark reminder of the realities of drinking. All peer to peer groups like this are fantastic because it allows those who have successfully quit to assist those who are struggling. But every good relationship goes two ways. Contact with those who are still drinking and are struggling keeps those who have stopped from forgetting the realities of their drinking years.

Some avoid social media when they quit drinking because they find it is littered with pictures of people drinking and memes that portray the harmless, fun and comical mask that we as a society put over the reality of drinking. Why do so many people find it necessary to post these images? In fact it is for the same reason that they like famous people and fictional characters who drink. This phenomenon is analysed and dissected in the next chapter.

## 6. Social Media and our Heroes and Heroines

This chapter is going to look at two seemingly separate aspects of drinking that in fact stem from the same cause. It is the need for drinkers to post pictures of themselves drinking (or even just their drinks) on social media and why drinkers have a tendency to like heroes and heroines (both real and fictional) whose appeal lies, to a significant degree, in their drinking.

Even people who have stopped drinking and are absolute happy to have stopped drinking and are 100% certain that they will never drink again will enthusiastically get involved in a conversation about their favourite drinking icons. People not only like to show themselves drinking but they also like to see people drinking. Think about Charlie Harper, Homer Simpson, Bertie Wooster, James Bond and WC Fields. Their drinking is a major part of their attraction. Think of the myriad of other people, both real and fictionalised (or often both) who we idolise, in no small part, because of their drinking.

Why do we like to see these heavy drinkers, both real and imagined, and why are we so keen to publicly display our own drinking?

One of the reasons for this is that we cannot see ourselves. Sure we get the odd glimpse in the mirror, but we can't actually step outside ourselves and really look at ourselves and see ourselves as other people see us. We can't meet up with ourselves and spend some time with ourselves and see what we are really like. So we do the next best thing, we interpret what we are like by looking at others that we think we are like, or even that we try to be like. We view ourselves in the same way we view others we think we are similar to, or have similar characteristics to.

This is why we love to sit down and watch Charlie Harper get up to his drunken shenanigans, or Homer Simpson, or WC Fields, and why we love to sit down and read about our personal idols and their drinking escapades. This explains the fascination for hard drinkers like Oliver Reed, George Best, and Richard Burton.

Someone emailed me and said the thing that triggered his stopping was he had been on holiday with his family and in the taxi to the airport on their way home his son had started talking to him about alcohol. He asked his son what effect he thought alcohol had on him. His son answered 'It makes you tired.' He had been thinking about his drinking for some time and at the airport after a quick Google search he downloaded and read Alcohol Explained. He stepped off the plane a non-drinker. One of the reasons something like this can have such a powerful effect on us is not so much that we suddenly realise what we are actually teaching our children but because children (up to a certain age) have absolutely no concept of other people's feelings, they have no concept of diplomacy; what they say is exactly how they perceive things. My eldest once asked me why I had a face like Spiderman and when I asked him what he meant he said because of all the lines on it. Another time he asked me why I had breasts. If an adult said the same thing I would think they were either joking or deliberately insulting me, either way I would assume these were the main motivators and would not necessarily think they genuinely perceived me in this way. But if a child says it you can be sure that this is simply how they see things. It is said without spite, malice or ulterior motive. If your partner said for example that drinking makes you look stupid you'd simply assume he or she was nagging you in yet another attempt to get you to cut down or stop, but if a child says it we believe them in a way we couldn't believe an adult.

The comments of children are one of the least distorted ways we can glimpse ourselves as others see us. It's not always what we want to hear. If you want a rude awakening and you have young children and you drink in front of them ask them what they think drinking does to you.

The problem with our drinking is that it makes us look like idiots, it degrades us and lessens us. Everyone knows that drinking makes them look pathetic, and we know it at a fairly deep level. The problem is of course that despite this we still want to drink because it makes us feel good, so we start looking at it from different angles to see if we can't see our drinking selves in a more favourable light. Our drinking icons are a classic way of doing this; we see ourselves in their image. We see ourselves in the images portrayed by James Bond, Oliver Reed, Marilyn Monroe, Ernest Hemingway, Bad Moms, Sex in the City, Richard Burton, The Macc Lads, George Best, Sean Penn, Winston Churchill, Olivia Pope, the list goes on. It is not that we necessarily think we are these people, but we see our drinking as they portray it; as comical, rebellious, elegant, tough, cultured, dashing, cavalier, reckless, or amiable. As opposed to the reality; pointless and degrading.

We spend a long time building up this distorted and enhanced image but a significant part of us knows on quite a deep level that this image we build up is sheer nonsense, which is why the comments of a child can burst this bubble in an instant, as can someone taking a photo of us or videoing us when we are drunk (Annie Grace actually recommends videoing yourself drinking and watching it). Like asking your children about what drinking does for you, it can give you a rude awakening.

This process actually goes two ways. We not only deliberately look to see ourselves in this romanticised and distorted way but we project ourselves in the same way. Hence our posting pictures of our drinking on social media. If someone is having a drink and a part of them is concerned about it, posting an image of it on social media can be a way of justifying it. If you have a glass of wine all on your own at 10am then clearly you have a problem, but stick a picture of it on Facebook with the comment 'it's midday somewhere in the world right?' or 'grape juice for breakfast' then all of a sudden it's funny, laddish, roguish, or whatever. Having a vodka and orange for breakfast means you have a serious drinking problem, but when Charlie Harper does it, it's comical, cavalier, even dashing. Getting up in the morning and immediately knocking back neat spirits is the very definition of alcoholism, but when James Bond does it, it's tough, gritty, and masculine.

Essentially, the phenomenon of posting drinking images on social media and our obsession with our drinking heroes and heroines both serve the same purpose; it is a way of justifying what we are doing, or normalising it, essentially it is a way of portraying it in a far more positive light. What you have is the same action, but two very different ways of interpreting it. It's not really surprising that we want to see it in the more positive light. After all, who would want to see themselves as a pathetic, helpless drug addict, when they can see themselves as a gritty, rebellious tough guy or a sophisticated independent woman?

Something to bear in mind is that we need to have a concern about something we are doing, we need to fear that it is wrong and weak to even make the attempt to portray it in a different light. This is why drinking memes, pictures of people drinking, and pictures of people's drinks are so prevalent on social media. A significant percentage of the population drink but an increasingly large number of these sense that it is a pointless and largely negative thing to do. So they seek to justify it and to portray it in a more positive light.

Fortunately this particular aspect of drinking is extremely easy to dismiss, you just have to look at the reality; it's all but bursting though the seams of the utterly unrealistic dressing we try to force it into (which is why an offhand comment by a child can explode it). The images we build up are frankly ridiculous and don't stand up to even the most cursory of examinations. Look at fiction. The general portrayal in films and on television are of people who spend almost all their time with a drink in their hand but it may as well be grape juice for all the effect it has. They never slur, stagger, look tired, get fat, or show in any way shape or form the physical effect of drinking. Occasionally you get an 'alcoholic' who knocks back entire bottles of spirits and drinks perfume and mouthwash if they can't lay their hands on alcohol. Finally you have the 'normal' characters who occasionally get fully drunk, usually because they are celebrating or have had something tragic happen. If you had never encountered alcohol and formed your view of drinking from TV, you'd assume alcohol had absolutely no physical effect for the first 4 or 5 drinks, then you suddenly went from stone cold sober to fully plastered with nothing in between. You'd also assume that unless you are compelled to drink 4 or 5 bottles of spirits a day you don't have a drinking problem.

The 'real' drinking icons are just as easy to dispel, but far more tragic when we scrape the surface. WC Fields said when he was close to death 'I wonder what it would have been like without alcohol?' Oliver Reed's legendary death in that bar in Malta was preceded by several months of sobriety (very much putting paid to the belief that he was a committed and unrepentant drinker), and the final weeks of George Best's life leaves absolutely no doubt that the reality of his drinking was a far cry from the image of him we like to use to justify our own drinking. Vivian MacKerrell (the real-life inspiration for Withnail from the film Withnail and I) was eventually unable to eat or drink anything due to the throat cancer that killed him at the ripe old age of 50, and resorted to injecting alcohol directly into himself through a syringe that was attached to a stomach bag. Near the end of his life he said to his father 'I never meant to be an alcoholic.'

The times are slowly changing and the mask of comedy, sophistication, rebellion, fun and happy times that alcohol has worn for so long is slowly slipping. More and more people are choosing not to drink and drinking is slowly going the way of smoking. But it takes time and for now you can expect to be bombarded with these false images. The problem is that in this age of mobile devices and social media we are bombarded with these images like no other time in human history. Just recognise them for the nonsense that they are. See the truth behind the façade and see the (often unconscious) insecurities that cause people to post these images in the first place. Before you start envying these people who post pictures of their idyllic lives on social media, remember that the grass is often greener on the other side because it's false.

## 7. Alcohol and Our Emotions

This is a key topic and one which, although I do cover in Alcohol Explained, I think would benefit from some amplification.

To summarise briefly alcohol is a chemical depressant which means that it depresses or inhibits nerve activity. So if we are upset, angry, or sad then a drink will depress these feelings with the result that, after a drink, we will feel slightly better.

The problem is that the depressant effect also acts on the limbic system which is a set of six inner structures in the human brain which is believed to be the emotional centre of the brain. It is believed that the function of the limbic system is to control our emotions and behaviour (and interestingly is also believed to be responsible for forming long-term memories). When alcohol depresses the function of the limbic system its ability to regulate our emotions decreases with the result that our emotions tend to run unchecked. This is why drunks tend to be overly emotional, be it angry, aggressive, sad, self-pitying, argumentative or regretful.

So let's now leave the science behind and look at a practical example. You have an argument with your partner and feel angry. You take a drink and feel better. The initial 'boost' (i.e. the deadening of the negative feeling of anger) is quickly countered by the brain which releases stimulants and stress hormones to counter the depressive effects of the alcohol. So you very quickly end up just as angry as before and need another drink to dampen the anger. And so the drinking continues.

You can probably already see the problem with taking a drink to relieve anger, stress, misery etc. The drinking has to continue for the relief to continue. However there are three additional problems that we need to factor in.

Firstly, due to the brain releasing a stimulant to counter the depressive effect of the alcohol, when the mental relaxation caused by the alcohol wears off we are not back to where we started. The stimulants remain with the effect that we are more uptight and stressed than before we started.

Secondly the mental deadening effect which provides relief from the anger dissipates far quicker than the physical intoxication. This is dealt with in Alcohol Explained but suffice to say that we become increasingly intoxicated as we chase the fleeting feeling of mental relaxation.

The third problem is that the physical intoxication affects the limbic system with the result that as we continue to drink our brains become increasingly unable to regulate our emotions (which in the case of the current example is anger).

The overall result of this is that we end up far angrier than we ever would have had we not drunk at all, which is an extremely important point given that we only started drinking to alleviate the anger in the first place.

It is easier to visualise this using the graph below which represents how angry we are over time. The vertical measurement is how angry we are, with higher being angrier. The horizontal line is time passing. As you can see the overall trend is for anger to increase. The short-lived dips are the immediate effect of taking a drink which does indeed take the edge off our anger. As you can see the relief very quickly wears off, and another drink is needed to obtain some more relief. But as the alcohol increasingly anaesthetises the limbic system, so we become increasingly incapable of regulating our anger with the result that our anger increases steadily overall.

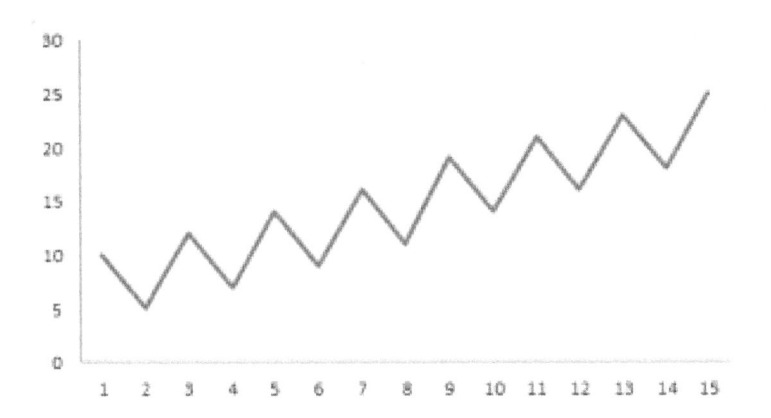

Each drink does provide us with an actual boost but this is outweighed entirely by the effect on the limbic system with the result that very soon we are far angrier than we were to begin with even while we are actually 'enjoying the 'relief' provided by the drink.

This touches on another topic covered in Alcohol Explained on the working of the subconscious. The subconscious is essentially that part of our decision-making process that is automated. It works on immediate cause and effect. If you take an action a hundred times with the same result your brain will trigger you to take the action when it perceives that the result is needed. The key is however that it only links cause and immediate effect. It will link the drink to the relief of anger because this is the most immediate effect, it won't link the drink with the overall increase in anger because this is a much slower process and is not therefore immediately obviously caused by drinking.

This is how we can end up with two totally contradictory core beliefs about drinking. Firstly, we all know that when you drink you get overly emotional be that emotion anger, regret, introspection, etc. Secondly we all instinctively reach for a drink when we are feeling angry, regretful, introspective, etc.

This is one of the many loose ends about drinking that, if you follow it along, allows you to unravel the whole sorry mess. After all, if alcohol did genuinely relieve anger, misery, frustration, etc, then alcoholics (who drink the most) would surely be the happiest people on the planet. Drunks would be the most calm and happy people, and those least likely to get into a fight. This is clearly not the case.

There is a very big difference between people drinking to relieve negative emotions (which they clearly do) and alcohol actually relieving negative emotions (which it clearly does not, in fact it does completely the opposite by greatly exacerbating them).

Emotions are a huge factor in many people's drinking, as are people's life circumstances. Their partner, their job, their lifestyle are all given as the reason people drink. We will examine this in the next chapter.

## 8. You Made me Drink

Most problem drinkers have a reason they drink, or several reasons. Their partner, their job, their kids, their past, their experiences, their life. It's not their fault. These things have happened to them and it drives them to drink.

In fact these are really just excuses. It helps to dissect this and analyse it fully using a classic example; it's my partner's fault that I drink. My partner is horrible, controlling, nagging, angry, they make my life a living hell. They drove me to drink. So let's go back to the beginning and look at this in a bit more detail.

Firstly all drinkers tend to drink to take the edge off the bad times. A bad day at work, kids playing up, an argument, something irritating or depressing comes along and they take a drink to anaesthetise it. Regular drinkers are already suffering from increased anxiety, tiredness and irritation that is part and parcel of long term regular drinking. Their starting point is one of irritability and anxiety. The normal stresses and strains of everyday life that non-drinkers take in their stride add to this anxiety. Drinking then relieves this, thus creating the illusion that alcohol helps instead of exacerbating the everyday ups and downs that are part and parcel of human existence on this planet. Very soon they have confirmed from personal experience what society has taught them about alcohol; that it relieves stress. So the more stressed and anxious they get, the more they drink. So if they are in a relationship that makes them unhappy then you can expect that they will drink more. But has that actually caused them to drink?

Remember that every human being on the planet suffers problems in one form or another and although most people in the Western world drink (some 86% of people in the US), worldwide only approximately half the population of the planet drink. That's an awful lot of people who manage to get through all the stresses and strains of life without having to rely on alcohol. And there's an increasing number of people in the West who now find that they can manage perfectly well without drinking. Take me for example. I spent 25 years relying on alcohol to get me through the bad times (and the good) but since quitting years ago I've managed far better without it.

The difference between the drinker and the non-drinker is that the drinker turns to alcohol when they hit a bump in the road, the non-drinker doesn't. And that choice; to turn to drink or not to turn to drink, lies with the individual alone.

A person may have as their life partner someone genuinely horrible. The partner may be argumentative, critical, bitter, negative, self-pitying and nagging. In that case the partner may genuinely be guilty of making that individual very miserable indeed. But it is the individual who has chosen to deal with that misery by trying to drink their way through it. That choice lies with the individual alone. They could choose instead to talk to their partner about the issues, leave them, do some exercise, go to counselling, speak to friends or family, read a book, go out to see a movie, or a million other things that could alleviate the misery. It is they and they alone who have decided to turn to drink. Part of that decision-making process may be subconscious and deeply ingrained, but it is still their responsibility alone.

This is true of any other problem they may face. Work, kids, bills, family arguments, anything, big or small. All of these things may cause you irritation or anxiety or misery and may be completely out of your control but when they happen you face a simple decision; drink to take the edge off them or use some other method to deal with them. This is why I find myself saying to people time and again that successfully giving up drinking isn't just about not taking a drink, it is about finding a new way to deal with stress and upset when they come your way, and they will come your way. Life is immeasurably better when you aren't drinking but it is still life, with all its ups and downs. Stopping drinking will make your life far better but it isn't going to miraculously solve all your problems.

Nothing forces you to drink, no person and no event can make you drink. Something or someone can make you unhappy, angry or upset, but it is you and you alone who decides to deal with that emotion by drinking. In fact it's an extremely poor method of dealing with life in any event. It provides only partial, slight and temporary relief, before magnifying any problems tenfold.

There is another aspect to this. I have been contacted by many people since first writing Alcohol Explained and a number of them have read, understood and fully agree with everything that is in it, but continue to drink because they consider that their lifestyles and personal circumstances are such that quitting just isn't a viable option for them personally. The following are real examples (anonymised of course):

Number one. Male in his 50s. He is a successful businessman running his own company. He works in a high-powered and stressful environment and is unmarried and has no children. He lives alone. He considers that his lifestyle dictates his drinking because he has no children or family which would give him a reason to quit drinking. He considers his financial situation (he has an excess amount of money) also exacerbates his drinking because he can afford to drink as much as he likes. He also considers that his stressful job contributes to his drinking because when he gets home in the evening he just wants to drink to escape from the stressful day. He has to socialise with clients a few times each week and considers alcohol to be an integral part of this.

Number two. Female in her early 40s. She has two young children. She considers that her drinking is caused by the stress of having a young family. She finds her two young sons extremely hard work and feels that her life is no longer her own. She considers these elements of her life prevent her from quitting.

Number three. Unemployed male early 20s. He considers that he drinks because he has no job, too much time on his hands, and feels worthless. He has very little money which causes additional stress and he feels that the relief provided by alcohol is the only pleasure he can get from life. He has no friends and no social life, and says he drinks to relieve his loneliness.

Number four. Male, mid 30s. He is employed but finds his job boring. He considers that he drinks to relieve boredom at work and finds when he is at work with nothing to do, the thing that gets him through the day is fantasising about, and planning, his evening drinking.

All of these are based on real people but I'm sure you can probably empathise with each of them and in all probability have experienced parts of each of their lifestyles and found that it has increased your drinking or discouraged your stopping. If one of these people sat down in front of you and told you about their lives and how it made them drink I'm sure you would be nodding in sympathy. Certainly most people in this society in which we live would listen to their stories and fully understand why they drink (if not condoning their drinking then certainly understanding how they are the victim of their circumstances and how this in turn leads to their heavy drinking).

But let's consider this in a bit more detail. We have people drinking because they have a job and people drinking because they don't have a job. Of those with a job, we have people drinking because their job is stressful and people drinking because their job is boring. We have people drinking because they have money and people drinking because they have none. We have people drinking because they have a family and people drinking because they don't. We have people drinking because they have too much time on their hands and people drinking because they don't have enough. There are people drinking because they socialise and people drinking because they don't.

Isn't it funny how alcohol always seems to win whichever way you slice and dice it? How it always holds the upper hand, pulls the strings, has the power? It's easy to see how people start to think of it as a sentient and evil being, how they see it as 'the demon drink'. Of course it's not that at all. It's just an inanimate chemical substance. It has exactly the amount of power that you decide to give it. Like a physically weak, but psychologically abusive, partner. The second you decide you've had enough and walk away, its insidious hold is gone. The only way it can retake its hold on you is if you start wanting it back again.

So is it really their lifestyles that are causing these people to drink? Or is it the fact that for years they have regularly been imbibing an addictive drug? Withdrawal from alcohol causes us to feel nervous and out of sorts, weak and scared. The drink then partially relieves that feeling and so we become fooled into thinking it is an essential part of our lives. Whatever we are doing, we need that drink to give us that little extra boost, to relieve that decidedly unpleasant feeling that can best be described as the loss of our mental resilience. It is essentially a feeling of not being able to cope with life and of being too easily overwhelmed by the stresses and strains which, without the withdrawal, we are able to take in our stride.

Your lifestyle is not the reason you drink or the reason you can't stop, it is just an excuse. Alcohol withdrawal and lack of sleep makes life seem stressful and difficult. Whatever life you have, the withdrawal makes it difficult and stressful. You can have a job or not have a job, be busy at work or be bored, you can have a family or not have a family, have a partner or not have a partner, whatever the circumstances of your life, with withdrawal makes it seem problematic and difficult and by then relieving the withdrawal it makes it seem manageable and even enjoyable.

Most people cannot change their lifestyles and even if a change is possible drinking will suddenly become just as crucial to your new lifestyle as it was with the old one. You'll still be miserable if you don't drink and 'happy' if you do (of course that 'happiness' is simply the feeling of mental well-being you get by relieving the withdrawal and is a feeling you would have all the time if you simply stopped drinking for good). What lifestyle change could possibly alter that dynamic? If you are looking at your lifestyle for the reason you drink and find it hard to stop you are looking in the wrong place. There's only one thing to analyse to understand why you drink and that's the nature of the drug itself.

We've previously touched on how, over time, our perception of our drinking years becomes increasingly idealistic and how this drags us back into drinking, but this is only part of the story. There is another ingredient required for the vast majority of people who return to drinking after a period of abstinence and that is the concept of 'moderation' and 'normal drinkers'. Most people don't start drinking again on the basis that they will drink like a fish and suffer hangovers, blackouts, relationship problems, health issues and financial detriment. So for this reason they firstly need to convince themselves that moderation or 'normal drinking' is a viable option for them. Indeed the single question I get asked the most is whether I think moderation is a long-term viable option. Let's now deal with this issue once and for all.

## 9. Moderation

Moderation seems to be an issue that is constantly coming up and I get asked regularly what I think about it. It very much links into the concept of 'normal drinkers' (as in 'can I be a normal drinker?') and why some people end up with drinking problems but others don't.

People who naturally have just one or two and then stop are invariable people who have never regularly drunk more than one or two and who consequently don't even consciously notice that insecure feeling building up when they've finished their drinks, let alone would they associate another drink with taking the edge off it. This is the key and it is also key that we who have travelled beyond that state can never go back to a state that is, ultimately, born of ignorance. Early stage drinkers can only maintain their intake at low levels because they don't consciously notice the small amount of anxiety that they experience after their one or two drinks, and / or it would never dawn on them to take another drink to get rid of it. The same is true when people start smoking, or taking cocaine or heroin. Every drug has a period where the user can seemingly take it or leave it. This period changes from drug to drug and from individual to individual but it is a progressive temporary phase and not a static state and, above all, it cannot be returned to. By this I mean that when you start taking a drug, any drug, there is a set period where you can take it or leave it before you become fully physically and psychologically addicted to it. But it is a one-time phase. When you have gone through it you can never go back to it. And it doesn't last forever. As soon as you take the first dose of the drug the clock is ticking. No one can ever know when they will become fully physically and psychologically addicted. Because alcohol is drunk instead of being snorted, injected or smoked it is one of the drugs that takes longest to become addicted to (this point is covered fully in Alcohol Explained in the chapter on The Subconscious). Also, because it's use is so widely condoned and even encouraged by society, many people can live and die without ever accepting that they are addicted to it. Many people don't enjoy social functions without drinking, others drink all or most evenings, many people drink from lunchtime, some even from the morning and drink virtually all day long, but still see it as a completely acceptable thing to do and would deny vehemently that they are physically or psychologically dependent on it. Alcohol is a drug that, for most people, takes a long time to become addicted to and even when addicted is very easy to deny that addiction for quite a considerable period.

What causes people to drink more or less than others is primarily due to environmental factors. Some people are brought up to just only ever have one or two drinks, others consistently drink to get drunk. This is what you learn from friends, family, colleagues, TV, music, etc and varies between individuals and even varies within the same family. Also some people's lifestyles allow them to drink more. So for me, I could never do my job under the influence of alcohol and I could never do it very well hungover, so for years that tempered my drinking. But if I didn't have to work or if I did a job where I could drink doing it I would have been drinking all the time (as I did when I had two months decompression leave upon my return from serving in Iraq).

Stress is also a big factor. Lots of these long-term moderate drinkers tend to have fairly simple, stress free lives. This is why drinking tends to be associated with high pressured and / or dangerous jobs. But stress isn't an objective test, it's subjective, so one person may find a certain lifestyle fairly easy to cope with, whereas someone else will find it difficult. So your ability to cope with stress, as well as how stressful your life is, is also a factor.

So why do I describe the 'take it or leave it phase' as a 'one time phase'? Is it really the case that a previously heavy drinker can never return to this moderate drinking state? I don't think it is possible to return to the 'take it or leave it phase' once we have passed through it for 2 reasons.

Firstly when you learn that the alcohol withdrawal can be relieved by another drink you can never unknow that. So forever after as soon as a drink wears off you will want another. The wearing off of one drink becomes the trigger for the next.

Secondly it's a catch 22 situation. To control alcohol you have to cease seeing it as something enjoyable. If you no longer want it you have power over it rather than vice versa. That is the only way it will lose its hold over you. If you see it as enjoyable or necessary you are going to keep wanting it. The only reason someone would want to moderate is because they still think of alcohol as enjoyable which means they are vulnerable. If you genuinely don't see it as enjoyable why on earth would you want to take it at all, moderately or otherwise?

Take me as an example. Sometime after I stopped drinking I took some Night Nurse not realising that it is 20% ethanol. It was the equivalent of having a small glass of port. Needless to say I realised my mistake and didn't have it again but I now know that theoretically I could have a single drink and not drink another because I did it on that one occasion. But here is the crux; I don't do that because I simply have no desire to drink anymore. If I did have that desire then I wouldn't be able to moderate because if I wanted one drink what would stop me wanting the next and the next and the next? The thing that allows me to take a single drink and then stop is the fact that I don't want to drink and never will (knowingly). If I did want a drink then I wouldn't be able to have just one because when that one drink was finished I would then want another. Drugs aren't like food, if you want a certain type of food and eat enough of it then you stop wanting it. With drugs the more you take them the more you want. That is their nature. And if I did have that desire to moderate, if I did have that desire to drink, I wouldn't be able to moderate because if I wanted a drink and had one what would stop me wanting the next and the next and the next?

Let me put it another way, if you think a single drink would be enjoyable, why on earth would the next one not be enjoyable? And the next and the next and the next? Remember alcohol is a drug, drugs create the need for the next dose. Moderation is based on seeing alcohol like a food, in that in taking it you remove the desire for it. So if you fancy a pizza and you have one. You are then full and content (or stuffed to bursting) and don't want any more. But alcohol doesn't work this way. When it wears off it leaves an unpleasant insecure feeling that needs another drink to get rid of it. This is the nature of drugs. I genuinely don't understand how anyone who has previously had problems with drinking could somehow teach themselves to want the first drink but not the next. I have no doubt there are some previously heavy drinkers who moderate but it can never be a stable state, it will always be reliant on them giving into temptation for the first drink or two then trying to resist that temptation for the next one. And as we all know the more drinks you have the harder it becomes to resist temptation.

Many people attempt moderation and some very few do manage to maintain it for some limited periods but what they find is that (surprise surprise) it isn't the nirvana they think it is. Drinkers don't like the drinking life. It's a life of tiredness, anxiety, lethargy, and even when they don't fully appreciate the extent of the mire that they are in they sense at a deep level that something unpleasant has taken hold of them. After all they used to enjoy life perfectly well before they started drinking, it's only after they've been drinking regularly for a few years that suddenly drinking becomes the highlight of their day, weekend, holiday, whatever and without it life seems flat. So they stop drinking, but then the effects of ambition start to take hold and they find that they're miserable having stopped and find themselves pining for a drink. They are miserable when they are drinking and they are miserable when they stop. So they look for a third option which is moderation. What they hope for is that by reducing what they are drinking they can have the good part of drinking but cut back on the bad. The problem is that 90% of the 'fun' of drinking is reducing the withdrawal and reducing the withdrawal for only 20 minutes a day is hugely more frustrating and hugely less enjoyable than relieving the withdrawal for hours on end. What they also invariably find is that they just end up spending their entire life obsessing about alcohol and thinking about when to drink and when not to drink.

I don't drink. Simple. Whether I go out for an evening and get offered a drink, or have a bad day, or go on holiday, or have a birthday, or meet old friends, or celebrate Christmas I don't drink. That is a given, it is not something I agonise over or repeatedly question or re-examine or look at from different angles to see if another solution will miraculously present itself. I've taken the time to examine alcohol, what it does for me and (crucially) what it does not do for me and I've made the decision not to take it ever again. Having made that decision I have then got on with my life. Alcohol as a chemical hasn't changed, my physiological and psychological make up hasn't changed, so the decision stands. Whatever happens I don't drink. I think about drinking a lot (hence this book) but I spend zero time considering whether to take a drink or not. But if I were to say to myself that I would drink in certain circumstances or within certain parameters, I would be spending all of my time thinking about whether I could or couldn't drink. I may or may not end up drinking all the time but my life would certainly be dominated by alcohol. I am a lawyer by profession. I know that no matter how simple and straightforward you make a rule there are always grey areas that are up for grabs. If there wasn't there would be no lawyers (and what a world that would be). No matter what your moderation rules are, there will be times that could just about fit into them or times when it seems reasonable to bend or break the rules. The reality of moderation for the previously heavy drinker is most likely failure but even if they do succeed for some limited period it's a time of frustration and spending great swathes of time agonising over whether to drink or not.

The other problem with moderation is that we assume that the less we drink the less of the bad side of drinking we get. Whilst this is certainly true to a degree it is not the case that it is directly proportionate. Remember, alcohol disrupts the delicate chemical balance of our minds and one of the knock-on effects of this is that our sleep is disrupted. This is as true for a single glass of something as it is for the whole bottle. The great feeling of sobriety is to let the chemical balance of your mind to return to normal and to sleep well and wake up feeling well rested and ready to go. One drink will stop you getting to that state so whilst cutting down can make you feel better physically, you are still a long way from being at your best and experiencing the very real joy of not drinking.

The other very important point to bear in mind is that for most people cutting back suddenly actually leaves them worse off physically than simply continuing at their usual level. If you usually drink a bottle of wine a night your brain is used to recalibrating in such a way as to increase the stimulant side of the scales to counter the alcohol in that bottle of wine. If you then one evening just drink one glass your brain is still recalibrating to counter a whole bottle with the effect that you are substantially over stimulated from that one glass. This is why long-term drinkers find that they don't sleep at all if they try to reduce their intake. It is the first drink that sends the message to the brain to start the recalibration process and the only way to avoid kicking off that process is not to drink. So everything on moderation in this chapter is also reliant on getting your brain used to drinking less which would require either a long period of abstinence and / or a period when you have one drink and suffer abysmally from overstimulation as a result of it until the brain gets used to the smaller amount of alcohol entering the system. Is this even possible? If so how long will this take? As far as I am aware no one knows. I am not aware of any tests being run on this area.

It is also worth mentioning that moderation in whatever form perpetuates the myth that alcohol is desirable and necessary in certain situations in order to fully enjoy and / or cope with them. If you say you want to moderate you are buying into that myth. You are saying that you cannot bear to think of living the rest of your life without this particular drug. If that's the position you're in have you beaten your addiction or does alcohol still have a hold over you? If it still has a hold over you, isn't it even more dangerous to dabble in it? Do you think heroin or meth addicts should moderate? Imagine if your son or daughter or father or mother or partner was hopelessly addicted to heroin and was close to dying from it but then managed to quit for an extended period. Imagine they then had a bad day at work or had an argument with their partner or were going out with old friends. Would you say to them:

"Why don't you inject a little bit of heroin? It'll be fine. Just have a little bit. A little bit won't hurt you. A little of what you fancy does you good. Oh go on, you're boring when you aren't comatose from heroin."

Why is alcohol different? And why would you give your loved one different advice to that which you would give yourself? The very concept of moderation denies that alcohol is an addictive drug.

Let me highlight another aspect that I think is important, that of responsibility for our actions. Let me give you an example. Imagine there is a drug that makes you go mad and kill people. Someone spikes your drink with this drug and unknowingly you drink it and kill someone. Are you morally responsible for that death? I would say no, because you had no intention to kill them and didn't choose to do so. It was the drug that made you do it and you didn't even choose to take that.

But what if you deliberately took the drug knowing that you would kill someone, and indeed did so? Would you be morally responsible for that person's death then? I would say of course you would be, you deliberately took the drug knowing it would result in a person's death. The key difference is choosing to take it or not. In one situation you didn't choose to take it and in the other you did.

But what if we now blur that line. Imagine if you deliberately took the drug but in the mistaken belief that it would just make you feel relaxed and happy for a few hours and didn't realise it would make you go mad and kill someone? You've actually chosen to take the drug but without realising its actual effect. My view is that in this situation you wouldn't be morally responsible for any deaths you caused while under the influence of the drug because you didn't intend anyone's death and it was in ignorance of this effect that you took the drug.

Drinking makes us tired, bad tempered, and likely to do stupid unpleasant things, but it's sold to us as something benign and fun. If you drink and do something terrible then my view is you shouldn't beat yourself up for that because society tells us that drinking is fun, sociable and (for most people) harmless.

But when you know through your own experience that you are capable of some quite unpleasant and irresponsible acts when you are drunk and you choose to drink anyway you've got to start taking responsibility for what you do when you are drunk. You may blur the moral lines of responsibility even further by convincing yourself that you can moderate and that this time will be different but the more times you prove yourself wrong on this the less you can absolve yourself of responsibility when you do horrible and embarrassing things when you've been drinking.

Alcohol is an addictive drug. Taking it creates the need for the next dose. For this reason moderation can never be a long term, stable condition. And even if it were you could never be better off moderating than quitting completely because quitting provides freedom. Moderation on the other hand simply ensures that alcohol continues to dominate your life.

At the beginning of this chapter I mentioned how moderation feeds into three distinct topics; moderation itself, why some people end up drinking more than others and normal drinkers. We've dealt with the first two of these topics, now let's consider the last; all those so called 'normal drinkers' that we problem drinkers are supposed to envy so much.

When looking at this topic the first thing we need to consider is 'what is a normal drinker?' In the UK that is a fairly easy topic to address because the government has done all the hard work for us. It has considered the topic in detail and liaised with all the important experts and come up with guidelines which, if you stay within, you keep health risks from alcohol at a low level. People who drink above these guidelines lose on average between 1 to 2 years of their life (Woods AM, Kaptoge S, Butterworth AS et al, The Lancet.

Published online April 13 2018 – yes I have finally quoted a reference).

This makes it nice and easy for us, after all if someone is drinking at such a level that they are losing a year or more of their lifespan through drinking they clearly aren't the happy, healthy 'normal drinkers' that we are so envious of because it is killing them. So what are these levels? They are a maximum of 6 pints of beer a week, or 6 small glasses of wine. However you shouldn't drink them all in one sitting (you should not drink more than two drinks in one day) and you should have several alcohol free days each week.

I have met many, many drinkers in my life and the only ones who naturally drank within these limits were people who didn't actually enjoy drinking. They didn't seem to like the taste or the effect but neither were they self-declared teetotallers. They would accept a drink if it was offered but it would never dawn on them to go out of their way to get some alcohol and when they did end up with a drink in their hand they didn't seem to particularly enjoy it. This is how one or two drinks can last them all evening; they aren't actually enjoying it to begin with. Forget alcohol for the minute, if someone gave you a really tasty soft drink, or some, really nice food, would it really take you hours to eat or drink it?

People who drink at these levels naturally, don't actually enjoy drinking. They either continue to not enjoy drinking in which case they will continue to drink within these levels or they will develop a taste for it in which case they very quickly find what every other committed drinker finds; that drinking within these levels is utterly unacceptable. In essence people who drink within these levels are just at the very earliest stage of the 'take it or leave it' phase of their drinking and as we've already covered, this is a (usually) short-lived stage that cannot then be returned to.

So if our criteria for 'normal drinker' is someone who is not substantially shortening their life through their drinking then we find that far from being normal, drinking at this level is in fact highly unusual and only exists short term, or exists because the drinkers themselves do not actually enjoy drinking. After all, if you genuinely enjoy something, why would you only want to enjoy it for half an hour or so a week, instead of several hours a day?

For the sake of argument and to make sure we are covering this topic off fully, let's change our criteria of 'normal drinker'. Let's say that we don't care about the UK government's guidelines about what we should drink (after all no one in the UK seems to pay any attention to them). Let's say we don't mind if we are cutting years or even decades off our life span and that isn't the criteria we are using when we refer to 'normal drinking'. Let's say our criteria for 'normal drinking' is that we can drink when we like, as much as we like, but that it isn't negatively affecting our lives to any great degree.

The problem is that alcohol does negatively affect our lives, even in small amounts (as we've already covered). The fact that the effects of it are so widespread that it is totally normalised doesn't affect this.

A healthy human being who is well rested and who isn't constantly interfering with the chemical balance in their brain will have an abundance of energy and the inclination to use it. Someone contacted me to say she had just stopped drinking and was on holiday with her partner and young son and although she wasn't drinking she missed having fun with her son. She said that mid-afternoon her partner would have a few drinks and start playing silly games with their son and having fun with him. That put me in mind of the many holidays I've been on where the adults come out in the morning and sit around by the pool while the kids come out and start going berserk from the off. The adults start drinking and after an hour or so start getting in the pool and playing with the kids. This again is one of those things that is now so normalised that we don't even question it. These are some of those 'normal drinkers' that we envy so much. The same is true of Christmas or family celebrations or even just weekends. The adults are tired and a bit grouchy but when the drinks flow the fun starts. However, there is an exception to this: me (and all other long-term non-drinkers).

Human beings are not designed to be tired and grouchy all the time and to only come to life and start having fun when they have a cancerous chemical sloshing around inside them. Feeling energetic, buoyant, positive, and ready to get out there and attack life should be your default state, a state that only changes if you are unwell or if some specific piece of ill fortune has befallen you. Holidays are a good example. Holidaying with a family is always fraught with issues and some arguments and moods are to be expected, but on the whole I'm in 'fun mode' from the moment I wake up until the moment I go to bed. 'Fun mode' is my default, not something that groggily raises its head for an hour or so each day, when I am in that very brief phase between drinking enough to get through the last withdrawal and tiredness, without yet having drunk enough to grind to a halt again.

Think about this so-called normal drinking. Imagine if you were on holiday with a big group of people who had never encountered alcohol, where all the adults were chatty and positive from the moment they woke up. Imagine if there then came among them a 'normal' drinker. Someone who was tired and grouchy and bleary eyed until they had their first drink. What would those people make of that individual? Just because the majority of people suffer something doesn't mean we should see it as 'normal' and it certainly doesn't mean we should envy them. If you envy a normal drinker you are envying them for the boost they get from their drinking but you then also have to envy them for the detriment that alcohol causes them because it is impossible to get the boost without the detriment. In fact the boost is part and parcel of the detriment because for the vast majority of people the 'boost' is just a partial and brief lessening of the detriment. What we are really doing when we envy 'normal drinkers' is to go through exactly the same process we go through when we look back fondly on our own drinking years. We build up an impossible fantasy, we create some ridiculous nirvana whereby we convince ourselves that some people can have a totally different experience of alcohol to ourselves. For them alcohol is what it ought to be; it gives them a wonderful boost without any particular downside, no corresponding anxiety, no disturbed sleep, no erosion of fitness, no lethargy, no arguments, no loss of memory, no weight gain and self-loathing. Of course the distorted image they post on their social media accounts that we are subject to on a daily basis just enforces all this. All those other drinkers have only the good side of drinking, they don't have any of the problems with it that we have, and we have their Facebook and Instagram photos to prove it!

Think of all the so called 'normal drinkers' that you envy. Are you telling me their sleep doesn't get disturbed when they drink? If they are a human being then that is not possible. If someone tells you that drinking doesn't disturb their sleep and that they feel fine the next day what they are really saying is that the disturbance to their sleep pattern isn't noticeable and this will either be because they don't wake up during the night (which does not mean that their sleep pattern isn't disturbed) or because they wake up all the time anyway. They are also telling you that their usual state is so far below par on a regular basis that the disturbed sleep caused by drinking leaves them feeling much the same. Is that someone to envy? The other message they are giving you loud and clear is that like the abused partner in the abusive relationship they are still at the stage of protecting and defending the abuser. People defend their drug of choice. One of the main steps in gaining freedom from a drug is to cease trying to defend your drug of choice and to start seeing it as it really is, as your enemy. If you have started to see alcohol as the enemy then the normal drinker should be the one envying you because you're one step closer to being free and obtaining all the wonderful benefits of sobriety than they are.

I don't envy normal drinkers because I'm the one who wakes up and feels good all day. Don't get me wrong, I have bad days, everybody does, but I don't turn good days into bad days by taking a poison that ruins my sleep and makes me feel tired and anxious. For me most days are good, some days are bad. That's life. For drinkers, normal or otherwise, any days after a night's drinking are bad, period. They may not have an actual hangover but even one drink spoils your sleep so even the one or two they drunk will have left them feeling tired and drained the next day. Hence sitting around waiting for the day to end instead of getting stuck into life.

Envy is never good but envying someone who is better off than you is understandable at least. But why would you envy someone worse off than you? Why would you envy someone who is tired when you aren't? Why would you envy someone who is only enjoying themselves as much as, and no more than, you? Particularly if their enjoyment is reliant on regular, expensive, doses of a drug? A drug that erodes their fitness and confidence, stops them sleeping properly, and makes them ill? What exactly is there to envy?

Imagine there's a weekly ten-mile hike. All the participants are all fit and strong, it always takes place on a lovely day and the walk is all through some beautiful scenery. In fact it's a wonderful and enjoyable experience. Only here's that thing, I've managed to convince a significant number of the participants (nearly 90% of them in fact) that they are only going to be able to manage the hike and more importantly enjoy it if they wear a certain type of hiking boot. In fact these boots are rubbish and they fall to pieces after about a mile and need replacing (but don't worry, I'll be there by the side of the road all the way ready and willing to sell them another pair). Because these boots are such poor quality although the walkers will just about be okay for the hike they are going to end up with some very bad blisters, sore legs and inflamed joints the next day.

*89*

Who would you actually envy in this situation? The 90% of poor fools who have been conned into believing that they need something they are far better off without, something that is costing them a fortune and actually hurting them considerably? Or the people that are happy to do the walk and enjoy it without having been conned into thinking that they need something that they don't?

What if there were a group of people who had done this walk a few times with these hiking boots, realised the error of their ways, and decided to do all future walks without them? Would you envy the people who were still being conned? Or those that had seen through the trick? Which group would you rather be in?

In fact the only thing I can think of that would make anyone want a pair of those 'special hiking boots' would be if everyone who was wearing them started banding together, and started exhibiting their blisters and swollen joints as a badge of honour, so that those lucky few who weren't wearing them started to feel excluded. But that would be a ridiculous situation, wouldn't it?

If, despite all I've said, you still envy 'normal drinkers' and still think moderation is a viable option then I have some good news for you; you can moderate if you want to. After all no one forces you to drink apart from yourself and no one can stop you from drinking if you want to. So if you want two drinks once a week or whatever you can do it. The choice is yours, but that choice has always been yours. So although it is theoretically possible to moderate you may want to ask yourself why you've not taken this supposedly perfect solution before. The simple fact of the matter is that you wouldn't be happy having two drinks a week or whatever it is you think would provide the good but not the bad. The fact is that those two drinks would simply awaken the desire for more so if you did have those two you would then be miserable because you couldn't have more, or you'd have more and end up absolutely getting increasingly intoxicated again and right back where you started. So the reason you are not a moderate drinker already is because there is no joy in it anyway, because it doesn't work in the way we convince ourselves that it should.

As I have mentioned, moderate drinking and the concept of normal drinking is a fantasy and like all fantasies when you start to analyse it evaporates. When we think about moderate drinking what we are really thinking about is something that we can have every now and then, that will make us happier, relax us, make us feel good about life and give us some relief from our worries, but that we won't then need to keep taking such that it leads to complete intoxication, hangovers, fatigue, self-loathing etc. Something that tastes nice, that we can do with friends, that will help us socialise and won't ruin our sleep, and above all it is something that has no downside. It sounds lovely and if you ever find such a thing please do let me know, I'll be the first to drink it with you! But the simple fact of the matter is that what I've described above isn't alcohol, in fact it's the direct opposite of everything that alcohol does; alcohol is the very antithesis of this. Alcohol never did and never can provide any of those things, you were just fooled into thinking it did. The more you drink the more you start to see the truth and once known the truth cannot be unknown. Imagine a relationship where you were head over heels in love with your partner and believed they loved you. You were deliriously happy for many years. Then you found out they really couldn't stand you, that they had never loved you and were cheating on you and mocking you behind your back and in fact doing whatever they could to hurt you. And in fact they weren't even attractive, they had just been wearing a clever mask and were in fact quite repulsive. Could you ever forget the truth and go back to them to get back to that period of happiness? Would you even want to knowing that it was all false? You might mourn the fact that you weren't in a happy relationship and you might look for one, but in respect of that particular relationship I would think you'd only be too glad to see the back if it.

In fact giving up alcohol is so much easier because you can find that wonderful relationship elsewhere. There is something that will make you happier, relax you, make you feel good about life and give you some relief from your worries, but won't lead to complete intoxication, hangovers, fatigue, self-loathing and won't ruin your sleep. A healthy mind and body will give you all of these things, and it is something you cannot fail to get if you stop drinking.

The final point we need to consider when dealing with moderation is could it be maintainable long term? Let's assume you can retrain your brain to react to the lessor amount of alcohol, and that you could somehow forget that another drink remedies the anxiety caused by the previous one (which logic dictates is impossible anyway). If you could get back to that state, could it be a state you could maintain long term? We already know the answer to this because we've experienced it before. We'd go through the same process as when we drank the first time which is to slowly (or quickly) increase our intake as our 'tolerance' (which is the name we use to describe the brain's ability to counter the depressive effects of the alcohol) increased. So even if you were to go through the painful process of reducing your tolerance the natural tendency would be for it to keep increasing anyway.

Now is a good time to cover something off that I didn't cover in Alcohol Explained, and that is the reason we as humans become addicted to so many various substances. This is to do with addiction generally rather than alcohol specifically but I think it is useful to cover this because it puts some of the topics that were covered in

Alcohol Explained (such as state and the working of the subconscious) into context.

# 10. Why do Humans Suffer From Addiction?

Allen Carr pointed out that one of the key aspects of the survival of living creatures is the ability to differentiate between poison and food. We use smell and taste to do this. Poisons like nicotine and alcohol taste and smell bad and we have to work at them until we become immune to the offensive smell and taste which then allows us to 'enjoy' the real pleasure of them which is the effect. What actually happens is that as we become immune to the foul smell and taste we find it easier to ignore it when getting our fix. This is what we mean when we refer to 'acquiring the taste' of something. I think this idea can be developed to give us a much fuller understanding of alcohol consumption and drug addiction generally.

Whilst living creatures do have an innate or pre-existing ability to differentiate between poison and food through smell and taste (i.e. one that is in their genes) they also have the ability to adapt it. After all very few (if any) species on this planet have a food source that is so reliable that they could never have any need to adapt it in times of scarcity. There are three aspects to this to consider.

The first aspect is that when we are drained, tired, hungry, etc a healthy nutritious meal will make us feel better, both physically and mentally.

The second aspect is that most substances on the planet that are 'poison' are not immediately fatal. Most of them, in the amounts we are likely to consume them, will leave us feeling ill rather than kill us outright.

The third aspect is that hunger increases the longer we go without food and the hungrier we get the more desperate we get. Most people in the Western world don't know true hunger. Most people eat three times a day and some people may skip meals and some even fast for various reasons but even then very few people go for more than a few days without eating. An otherwise healthy human being can survive for a month to 40 days without eating. Imagine how hungry you get after a few hours not eating. Imagine how desperate you would get after a few weeks. That desperation will cause living things to eat virtually anything as they become increasingly hungry.

So where do we get to if we consider all of these aspects together? To survive on this planet all animals must have the ability to adapt their diet. So if their normal food supply runs out they will become hungrier and hungrier, eating whatever is available. If they consume something that they wouldn't ordinarily want to eat, or something that tastes or smells offensive, and they feel immediately better after they consume it (for example if it relieves hunger or tiredness) and providing it doesn't make them immediately ill, on a subconscious level their brain will conclude that what they ate actually had some form of nutritional benefit i.e. that it is 'food' rather than 'poison' and as it didn't seem to harm them they can continue to consume it. As such, over time, they will cease to be repulsed by the smell and taste of it and instead will start to find it appetising and will even start to hunger for it. In this way if a living creature's food source becomes scarce or disappears they will be able to adapt to other food types through trial and error. This is a key element to survival. Take something foul but obtain an immediate benefit from it and your brain will reprogram itself to see it as desirable rather than poison to be avoided, and in time you will even hunger specifically for it.

As a child I found the smell of Stilton (a very mature blue cheese) repugnant. I remember seeing my Father eat it and wondering how anyone could want to eat something so vile. However I used to have a very watered down version of it by having soup with a small amount of it crumbled in. I also kept trying it on the odd occasion. Now I eat it quite happily, in fact I 'like' the flavour of it. The smell and taste remain the same, they haven't changed, it is just that on a subconscious level my body and brain has realised that it doesn't make me physically ill and it also relieves hunger. Thus I became able to eat it and even, eventually, to enjoy it.

This is a great system and one that ensures our survival but where it falls down is in relation to drugs. A drug can make us feel immediately better but not because it has nutritional benefit but because it interferes with our chemical functioning such that we feel better even though the actual physical effect is a negative one.

This is one of the reasons that studies showing the supposed benefits of consuming alcohol are so readily accepted. On a deep level drinkers truly believe alcohol is good for them. It makes them feel better. They feel nervous and anxious and out of sorts and they take a drink and then feel confident, calm and positive. These studies are always hugely flawed but drinkers flock to them not only because it justifies what they are doing but also because they find it very easy to believe. It is something that they already 'know' to be true through their own experience.

This is fairly straightforward when we have the basics in place but unfortunately like many things to do with addiction and alcohol it tends to become an area of general misunderstanding and confusion. One of the reasons for this is the fairly recent discovery of several naturally occurring drugs (i.e. drugs that are created and secreted by the brain) and the role they play in addiction. The three best known of these are dopamine, serotonin and endorphins.

Dopamine is essentially a chemical that motivates you, it makes you want to do something. It makes you feel like you want or need something. Your body releases it when you drink because it counters the depressive effects of the alcohol. When you have a drink you tend not to care about things; you don't bother about clearing the kitchen before bed, doing the washing, cleaning up, or the myriad of other things that, if you weren't drinking, you wouldn't be able to leave.

The problem is that this 'not caring' is not your natural state. Your brain recognises that your motivation levels are low so it increases dopamine to get you moving again. You then go to sleep, the alcohol wears off, but the excess dopamine remains.

This is why a lot of people find that the day after drinking (provided they haven't drunk too much) they wake up and want to eat or have sex. This is caused by the dopamine. Your sex drive goes up, appetite goes up, in fact you will have a much greater motivational need to obtain virtually anything you can think about (even more alcohol). This is why trying to control what you eat after a night's drinking is virtually impossible and is one of the many reasons drinkers tend to be overweight. The increased dopamine makes them constantly want to eat even if they aren't hungry or even if they are actively full.

I emphasise here that this is the position when you are drinking at lower levels. When you reach a certain point the left-over stimulants are such that your appetite decreases. Generally speaking depressants increase appetite and stimulants decrease it. This may seem counterintuitive but it isn't if you factor in that digestion takes huge amounts of energy (which is why we feel sleepy after a large meal). Your body wants you to eat when you are physically inactive so it can divert resources to digestion. It doesn't want you to eat when you are likely to have to then engage in physical activity. So the chemicals that your brain releases when you are relaxing (the depressants) make you want to eat and the chemicals it releases when you are going to have to engage in physical activity (the stimulants) decrease your appetite. So at lower drinking levels the dopamine overrides the stimulants and makes you overeat, at higher levels the increased stimulants make eating difficult if not impossible.

Serotonin and endorphins on the other hand are chemicals that make us feel good. Alcohol consumption has been linked to an increase in these and so there is an assumption that one of the chemical effects of alcohol is to increase the levels of these feel good chemicals which creates a feeling of euphoria. People will often say that drinking causes the brain to release serotonin and endorphins and therefore say that drinking alcohol will always result in a feeling of euphoria, but in fact there's absolutely no evidence that it is the direct chemical effect of the alcohol that is responsible for the increased levels.

There is much that we as humans do not know about these chemicals and how they affect us (or indeed what other chemicals may play into the equation which are yet to be identified) but what is becoming increasingly clear is that serotonin and endorphins are survival chemicals, and by this I mean that they contribute towards the survival of the individual, the family unit, and the species. When you do something that is good for you personally or good for the species you are rewarded with a boost of these and this in turn makes you feel good. So eat something, do some exercise, have sex, interact socially with others, and you get this feel good boost. In this way the human species is encouraged to increase and flourish.

Of course the human brain is far more complicated than this. Did you know that decreasing stress can raise the levels of serotonin and endorphins? Stress will actually decrease the levels and removing stress can increase it. Remember that alcohol withdrawal and tiredness (both by-products of drinking) are a form of physical stress. Alcohol will remove both of these forms of stress by relieving the withdrawal and anaesthetising the tiredness. Your body will interpret this as 'beneficial'. In essence is can be tricked by the effect of the drug.

It is also worth bearing in mind that often we drink while also eating and / or socialising so this feel good boost is often due to these two aspects rather than the drug itself. If you are in any doubt about this try drinking at home, alone, with no tv or radio or other distractions. See if you feel euphoric or just slightly dulled and confused.

If alcohol simply had the chemical effect of releasing serotonin and endorphins then every time you took a drink you'd be euphoric. Clearly this isn't the case. Some people suggest that over time your brain reacts to the constant release of these feel good chemicals by no longer releasing them in response to alcohol, but if this were the case then you would never experience any pleasure while drinking and this clearly isn't the case either. In fact what we find is exactly the same that we found during our whole drinking lives; that sometimes a drink really makes us feel good but other times it seems to do nothing at all. This is because it is the circumstances and not the alcohol itself that leads to this 'feel good' boost. Of course you will experience less and less pleasure from drinking over time because over time the negative effects of drinking become more and more apparent and we tend to worry about our drinking more and more. After all, you're not going to get your 'feel good boost' if you are worrying about something. This in and of itself will ensure that you get less serotonin and endorphins when you are drinking and is another reason why, over time, our drinking becomes less and less enjoyable.

As I mentioned at the beginning of this Chapter this aspect applies to all drug addiction not just alcohol and I think it is best highlighted by using dipping tobacco as an example. For those not familiar with dipping tobacco, it is a form of chewing tobacco that is very finely shredded and moistened. It is mostly consumed in the US and some Scandinavian countries. You take a pinch of it and tuck it between your gum and your cheek and the nicotine is absorbed into bloodstream through your mouth. By making various chemical changes to it the manufacturers are able to ensure that the maximum amount of nicotine is absorbed as quickly as possible, thus making it even more addictive than normal chewing tobacco. As you would expect it is highly cancerous and with regular use it burns through your gums and cheek. Aside from causing mouth cancer it can also eventually leave holes in the cheek.

This begs the question, 'doesn't it hurt?' After all if you are putting something in your mouth that burns through your skin doesn't it sting? I can speak from personal experience because when I was younger I lived in a house share with an American who used to dip and I became addicted to it for a period. I can tell you that you do feel it burning but that it actually feels quite nice. For those who have never experienced dipping tobacco you are probably wondering how a burning, stinging sensation in the mouth can feel nice. The reason for this is that your brain starts to link the burning sensation in your mouth with the relieving of the nicotine withdrawal. The feeling remains the same but the way your brain interprets it changes. It starts to become desirable instead of unpleasant. The mechanism for nicotine withdrawal is outside the scope of this book but suffice to say that nicotine is a powerful stimulant and the brain seeks to counter it using much the same principles that are at play when countering the depressive effects of alcohol. Nicotine withdrawal is unpleasant and leaves you feeling out of sorts and less able to cope with the usual ups and downs of everyday life. When you put nicotine inside your bloodstream you are relieving this unpleasant feeling which leaves you feeling more confident, resilient and positive. So your brain starts to interpret the burning, stinging feeling in your mouth as a good thing, which in turn enables you to keep doing it until you burn a hole in your face and contract mouth cancer.

This may seem odd to anyone who has not tried dip but if you think about it the principle is exactly the same with smoking. Breathing smoke into your lungs is not natural or enjoyable and if you don't believe me then next time you are near a bonfire or barbeque get nice and close and take a big lungful of the smoke. Many people when they start smoking cough and splutter and it takes time for them to 'get used to it' or 'learn to enjoy it' or 'develop a taste for it'. All these things mean that your brain starts to reinterpret an experience in the light of an unexpected response. Usually we would interpret something like a stinging feeling in our mouth, or breathing in a lungful of poisonous fumes, as deeply unpleasant, but because of our innate ability to adapt to changing circumstances and environment our brain is able to re-categorise experiences as enjoyable and desirable because they appear to confer an actual benefit. Eventually the brain will trigger a hunger or desire for the cause' (in this example breathing in poisonous fumes or putting something in our mouths that burns and stings) when the effect is required (i.e. the withdrawal needs relieving).

Exactly the same principle applies to drinking alcohol. Alcohol is a poison, it kills living things (which is why it is used as a disinfectant) and we are preprogramed to find the smell and taste repulsive. When we drink it, it smells horrible, it tastes horrible, and it can burn our mouths and stomach. However very soon our brain starts to reinterpret all of these things as beneficial as it learns that alcohol relieves tiredness, anxiety, anger, etc. As we've already covered in some detail it actually does none of these things. What it really does is to cause tiredness, anxiety, anger etc but then partially relieves them. But the unconscious part of the brain works purely by cause and effect. It will recognise that alcohol relieves tiredness, anxiety hunger etc because you will take a drink, experience the foul taste and burning sensation and shortly after this you will experience the relief. That is the immediate effect. It will not link the burning and foul taste with the causing of these problems in the first place because these are the long term, rather than the immediate, effect. So the taste of the alcohol, the burning feeling in our throat, chest and stomach as we drink it, all start to become interpreted as pleasurable. The 'warming' feeling of a drink is actually the feeling of a carcinogenic chemical burning our living body.

The human body and brain is a phenomenally advanced and adaptable survival machine but it can be tricked by the effect of drugs which appear to confer benefits when they are in fact extremely detrimental to our physical and mental health in both the long and the short term.

The link between hunger and addiction and drinking of course leads to the sometimes controversial topic of stopping drinking and losing weight.

# 11. Stopping Drinking and Weightloss

Why is the topic of stopping drinking and weightloss controversial? It is because whenever anyone mentions the weight they lost when they quit drinking there always seems to be a significant number of people who say that they quit drinking and didn't lose any weight, or even that they gained weight. I cover this topic in Alcohol Explained but now let's go over it again and include some new aspects so as to put the issue of drinking and weightloss to bed once and for all. Firstly let's just briefly recap on the main points that were covered in Alcohol Explained:

### 1. Empty calories

The first and easiest one, alcoholic drinks contain a huge amount of empty calories. A single pint of beer averages out at 182 calories (roughly the same as a slice of pizza), which you will need to run for 18 minutes to burn off. A large glass of wine contains 318 calories which you'll need to run for 32 minutes to burn off. And let's be honest, who stops at just one? Bearing in mind most people need around 2,000 to 2,500 calories a day, you can see how those extra calories from drinking soon build up.

### 2. Alcohol as an energy source cannot be stored

Aside from the actual sugar in alcoholic drinks the alcohol itself is an energy source but one which humans cannot store as fat. Because your body cannot store it, it has to burn it off. This is one of the reasons we quite often get hot when we are drinking; it is the excess alcohol energy being turned into heat energy. The problem is that because your body already has excess energy from the alcohol which it is struggling to rid itself of virtually every other calorie you consume from another source gets stored as fat.

### 3. Appetite stimulant

Alcohol is an appetite stimulant which means it makes you feel hungrier than you actually are. As I've mentioned previously depressants can increase appetite (unless of course you end up totally incapacitated, as is often the case with heroin addicts). It is also the case that hunger can come from lack of available energy or lack of nutrients. If your hunger is from lack of nutrients you will usually fancy something healthy and nutrient rich. Because alcohol simulates the hunger from lack of available energy we tend to crave calorie dense fast food rather than healthy alternatives.

### 4. Dulling of receptors that tell you when you are full

Alcohol is an anaesthetic and a depressant (i.e. it anesthetises or 'depresses' nerve activity). It depresses / anesthetises receptors that tell you when you are full, leaving you more able and likely to overeat.

### 5. Vitamin deficiency

Alcohol inhibits absorption of certain key nutrients like vitamin B-9, vitamin B-12, thiamin, calcium, iron, zinc, and other fat soluble vitamins such as vitamins A, D and E. This leads to an almost constant hunger as the body constantly triggers the feeling of hunger to obtain the vitamins that it is lacking.

### 6. Fitness erosion

The stimulants that are released when you are drinking cause your heart rate to speed up without any associated physical activity. When we exercise our muscles require more oxygen so the heart speeds up to keep up with the increased demand by our muscles for oxygen and nutrients. Over time the red blood cells become more concentrated and also have a shorter life span so that they are younger (those that are younger are more efficient at carrying oxygen and nutrients) thus each pump of the heart delivers more nutrients and oxygen. Of course the converse is also true. If we are regularly pushing our heart rate up without any related physical activity then each pump of the heart is delivering too much oxygen so the red blood cells will space out and their life span will increase and consequently they will carry less oxygen. It is the reverse of getting fit; it is a way of actively becoming unfit.

### 7. Sleep disruption

As covered previously alcohol disrupts our normal sleeping pattern meaning we do not get the quality sleep we need. As a consequence we are left feeling tired and lethargic the next day and less inclined and less able to exercise. Tiredness also causes increased hunger as our bodies try to compensate for the lack of sleep by obtaining more readily available energy.

### 8. Testosterone

Alcohol causes a decrease in testosterone which in turn leads to increased body fat and decreased muscle mass. To say nothing of erectile problems, hair loss, mood swings, and fatigue.

For all these reasons it seems reasonable to conclude that if you cut out alcohol you will immediately start losing weight but this isn't necessarily the case. Firstly let's get the basics in place. You lose weight by burning up more calories than you consume. It really is that simple. All these fad diets and fitness routines can't get around that one concept. It's simple physics. Energy you consume is either stored or burned off. To put it another way if you burn off more calories than you consume then you lose weight and if you consume more calories than you burn off then you gain weight.

So if you need 2,500 calories a day, and you are consuming 3,000 calories of food and 1,000 in alcoholic drinks, and you cut out the alcoholic drinks you won't lose weight. Even without the 1,000 calories of alcohol you are still consuming 500 more calories than you're burning up.

But the fact is that the vast majority of people who quit drinking don't consume the same amount of calories in food that they consumed when they were drinking, they consume more. They treat themselves to cake, chocolate, fast food, etc. That is absolutely fine in the short term, you deserve to cut yourself some slack now you've quit drinking, but the fact is that if you do this you aren't going to lose any weight.

Lots of people when they quit drinking try to incorporate some kind of fitness routine (particularly if one of their motivators for quitting is to lose weight and let's face it, who doesn't want to lose a bit of weight?). That is a fantastic thing to do. One thing I didn't cover in Alcohol Explained that I have found myself saying on innumerable occasions is that quitting drinking isn't just about cutting out alcohol, it is about finding another coping mechanism when times get tough, as they invariably do. Sober life is immeasurably better, but no life is perfect.

One of the things about alcohol is that, because it anaesthetises, we tend to use it as a method of stress relief. When you quit drinking you become massively more able to cope with life's ups and downs but everyone has really bad times and during those times it is natural to look for something to give you a boost or some solace. When you have been drinking for several years you are very used to reaching for something to put in your mouth to consume to give you that boost. If you don't have a plan in place there can be a distinct tendency to just reach for the next thing to consume now that alcohol is no longer available. For many people the obvious replacement is food so they start emotional eating. Hence not only do they not lose weight when they quit but they may even gain weight. This is also one of the reasons some people think they have addictive personalities; they give up one addiction merely to end up with another. In fact the reality is that they have simply given up one thing without making a plan to deal with future stress and thus just end up reaching for the next thing when times get tough. They retain the learned reaction that, when confronted with any form of stress or discomfort, they reach for something to put inside them to change their mood.

There are many, many things you can use when times get tough. Reading, a nice meal, time with friends, a film, meditation, yoga, exercise, the list goes on. Personally I primarily use exercise and reading. Exercise is a fantastic stress reliever, it releases endorphins and serotonin and the only side effects are fitness, weightloss and better sleep. However even this can have its pitfalls from a weightloss perspective. People who incorporate an exercise routine when they quit are often even more annoyed if they don't lose weight. But remember you only lose weight by burning off more calories than you consume. Even if you are doing so much exercise you are burning off 10,000 calories a day you still won't lose weight if you are eating 11,000 calories a day. And remember, your body triggers that feeling of hunger when you are getting low on calories so even if you are exercising at a very high level, all that will happen is that you'll be hungry all the time so you will end up eating more and more.

There is another aspect to drinking and weight that I didn't cover in Alcohol Explained and that is the effect of dopamine. As covered previously dopamine is one of the chemicals your brain releases to counter the effects of the alcohol so when the alcohol wears off you end up with an excess of it. It increases your motivation for things like food and sex which is why we tend to be extra hungry after drinking. This in turn leads to overeating and the problem with overeating is that it becomes easier and easier to do. Stop for a moment now and think about your clothes. How often are you aware of the feel of your clothes? I don't mean how you feel wearing them but how they feel against your skin. If you concentrate you can feel them but the vast majority of the time you aren't conscious of them. Even if they are too tight or are in some other way uncomfortable often we soon cease to be consciously aware of them. This is because when there is something physical that we experience all the time or for long periods we cease to be consciously aware of it.

Think of hunger as a scale of one to a hundred, with one being absolutely ravenous, and a hundred being so full you can scarcely move. Assume that for most people a comfortable place to exist is between 40 and 60. So at 40 they become a bit hungry, and at 60 they are nicely full. If they start regularly eating between 70 and 80 (at which point they are starting to become uncomfortably full) that soon becomes the norm and the feeling of fullness is with them so often they cease to be aware of it and when it starts to disappear they start to interpret that as 'hunger'. In this way overeating, like drinking alcohol, is progressive and tends to increase over time. Regularly having too much dopamine means you are regularly overeating which makes overeating easier and easier as we become immune to how full we are really feeling. Even intermittent binge drinkers suffer from this because even overeating once or twice a week increases the ability and tendency to overeat over time. If you are drinking at the weekend only you are spending two days out of 7 drinking, but the dopamine remains for two to three days after that which means you are overeating 5 days out of seven. When you quit drinking and start to live without the constant excess dopamine there is a natural tendency to start eating slightly less over time and also to return to a healthier diet. By this I mean that instead of having regular and very strong cravings for fast food your desire for them will slowly decrease over time. You will fancy unhealthy, high calorie food less and less and find it easier and easier to resist.

Another point I need to add to this topic that wasn't in Alcohol Explained is the issue of salt. Salt has quite a bad reputation at the moment and the generally accepted consensus is that you should avoid it. This is a contentious issue and this view is not shared by all experts in the field by any means. Many people actually think that salt is in fact good for you and that we should be eating more of it. One of the reasons the topic of salt is controversial is that all the studies that the experts use to show that salt is bad for your heart are studies that just show trends rather than cause and effect. By this I mean that the studies show that people who consume more salt tend to have more cardiovascular problems. The problem with studies of this sort is that it is possible that it is not the salt that is the cause of the increased cardiovascular problems but some other lifestyle aspect could be to blame.

Fortunately we don't need to get bogged down in the academic technicalities of it because what is unarguable is that too little salt causes problems. Hyponatremia is when a person's sodium (salt) level in their blood drops too low. It can cause headaches and nausea. One of the causes of this is drinking too much liquid. Any liquid you drink eventually comes out and with it comes small amounts of salt (be it by way of urinating or sweating). When you drink more liquid, you lose more salt.

When you drink alcohol you are consuming liquid for the effect of the drug and not because you are thirsty. Mostly you would never consume that amount of liquid if there wasn't alcohol in it. Even if you are really thirsty a pint or so of water will usually stop your thirst. You would never sit there and drink glass after glass of water, particularly if you weren't even thirsty to begin with. The reason we can do this with alcohol is because over time we become conditioned (or reconditioned) to drink for the effect. This takes us back to the point we covered in the chapter about why humans are vulnerable to addiction. It's exactly the same mechanism as starting to enjoy the feeling of having dipping tobacco burning through your cheek, or breathing in cancerous smoke. Because each drink gives you a boost and relieves the anxiety that is slowly building up from the last drink, your brain starts to trigger you to keep taking a drink even though by doing so you can cause yourself serious problems from a salt deficiency perspective. If you are in any doubt about this sit yourself down and try to drink the volume of liquid you usually consume when drinking alcohol but consume it as water. You will soon find, particularly if you are a beer drinker, that you feel physically repulsed at the thought of drinking another drop. This is your body protecting you against hyponatremia. The fact that you can drink that amount of liquid when it is alcoholic is a further example of how your brain has been tricked by the drug into allowing you to do something harmful.

From a weightloss perspective you just need to factor in the fact that when you are low on salt your body will trigger salt cravings. When you are drinking and during the day after you have drunk you will want to consume large amounts of salty food. Often these foods tend to also be high in fat and high in calories, such as cheese, processed meat, crisps / chips, and fast food.

Personally I do wonder whether the studies that show people who eat more salt are more prone to cardiovascular issues have been misinterpreted and it is the alcohol consumption and associated poor diet that is causing the problem rather than the salt.

Be that as it may there is one final topic that needs to be covered off when we are considering the issue of drinking and weightloss and that is heart rate. As touched on previously your heart pumps blood around your body and the blood carries oxygen and essential nutrients to your muscles and organs. If you increase your physical activity then your heart needs to pump faster so that more blood (and therefore more oxygen and nutrients) can reach your muscles to keep up with the increased demand. If you increase your heart rate regularly through exercise your blood cells carry more oxygen and nutrients, and also become more concentrated, so that each pump of the heart delivers more oxygen and nutrients. If you regularly increase your heart rate without exercising (for example by taking drugs) the opposite happens. Your muscles and organs end up with an excess of oxygen and nutrients, so your blood cells start to carry less and become less concentrated. This is why resting heart rate (counting the number of times your heart beats in a minute) is considered a good indicator of health and fitness; the lower the count the fitter you are. This much was covered in Alcohol Explained but there is another aspect to this worth mentioning.

The human heart can only beat so fast. The usual formula used to work out your maximum heart rate is to subtract your age from 220. Of course this isn't a particularly scientific approach and no doubt there will be differences between individuals but the fact is that the human heart has a maximum speed at which it can beat. If you are exercising at a level that you can't keep up with, to such an extent that your muscles are using oxygen faster than they can be supplied, then eventually you will faint due to lack of oxygen in your blood. But your body doesn't just let you merrily exercise away until you faint. As your heart increases it produces a level of discomfort that makes you want to slow down, to stop, to sit down and to rest. This is a key point to keep in mind; the faster your heart is beating the more you want to slow down and rest.

The next point we need to move on to is a concept we have covered earlier; that alcohol is a chemical depressant and that your brain seeks to counter its effects by increasing the stimulant side of the scales. We have also covered how stimulants speed us up and make us more alert and depressants slow things down. You would be forgiven for thinking that alcohol as a depressant slows your heart rate down but in fact most of the time it doesn't. Your heart will often need to beat faster, for example if you are undertaking increased physical activity or anticipating such activity (which is why your heat rate increases when you are scared as your brain anticipates a 'fight or flight' response). For this reasons drugs (both those naturally occurring in our bodies and those that are not) can increase our heart rate dramatically. But your heart never has a reason to drop below its natural, resting heart rate, so depressants generally speaking will never drop your heart rate to any significant degree (unless we really overdose on them). So when you are drinking you don't get a decreased heart rate which the stimulants then return to normal, you get a normal heart rate which the stimulants increase (both during and after drinking). So as far as heart rate goes it's all bad, with increases and no decreases. Your heart rate can slow down with depressants but you need to take a significant amount of a type that your body is not familiar with for this to take effect. For the majority of people who are drinking the amount that they usually drink ,the effect is an increased heart rate both during and after their drinking (with the increase after drinking being far more pronounced).

Any doubt about this aspect of drinking has been totally dispelled by the prevalence of fitness trackers. I'm sure most people reading know what I am referring to when I mention fitness trackers but for those unfamiliar with them they are bands you wear on your wrist, very much like a watch, that measures your heart rate, sleep, and the number of steps you take in a day. As we've covered it is the alcohol withdrawal that causes the increased heart rate. If someone were to drink alcohol and have no withdrawal, then (alcohol being a depressant) you would expect their heart rate to slow down and their sleep to be deep and long. All the data from fitness trackers show a very different story. They invariably show increased heart rate and a very fragmented sleeping pattern. If you own a fitness tracker and are still drinking it is worth comparing the drinking data with the non-drinking data. The results can be startling.

So two main points to bear in mind here; when you drink your heart rate increases (both during and after the drinking) and when your heart rate increases you want to sit down and rest. In this way drinking makes us feel tired and lazy; we become far more inclined to want to sit down and rest when we are drinking and this tendency is even more pronounced the following day when much of the alcohol has worn off and the stimulants hold sway. This contributes to that horrible feeling you have the day after drinking of feeling both tense and restless, but also tired and lazy at the same time. Of course you get people who exercise after drinking but they tend to be fit anyway and they will be exercising at a far lower level and will be finding it much harder work than if they hadn't drunk at all. If, for example, your resting heart rate is 60 and your maximum heart rate is 180 then you have a 120 potential increase. But if your resting heart rate is 60 and your maximum heart rate is 180 but you've been drinking and your heart rate is already at 100, you've only got an 80 potential increase. Not only that but if you are starting at 100 you are already feeling weak and inclined to sit down and rest before you've even started exercising.

This aspect doesn't just impact your weight, it has a huge impact on your quality of life for both regular and binge drinkers. The excess stimulant phase usually lasts 24 to 48 hours after drinking so one fairly substantial drinking session will have you operating at reduced levels for around 3 days. So even if you're only drinking once a week nearly half your time is spent way below where you ought to be and of course is also eroding your fitness generally. I have more energy now in my 40's than I did in my thirties, twenties, and even teens. So many people put their increasing lack of energy down to age but for many people it's the drugs that they take on a regular basis (like alcohol and tobacco) that cause this feeling. They increase your heart rate which makes you feel lethargic and tired. Getting back to a natural state is like putting down a 60lb back pack that you've been wearing all day every day for years on end.

The overriding point to take away from this chapter is that quitting drinking does not guarantee weightloss but it does provide the opportunity for it. It makes exercising easier, it makes eating smaller meals easier, and it makes healthy eating easier.

## 12. Drinking Myths and Platitudes

There are a few platitudes around drinking that I think we need to dispel. These are comments or phrases that you hear all the time, some of which can be quite damaging. We can't stop people using them but we can lessen their negative effect by not taking them for granted and by shining the light of reason on them and showing them to be the nonsense they are. I am not going to deal with all of them, there are too many. Also I am not going to bother wasting time on those that are clearly nonsense (such as those in the 'a glass of red wine a day is good for you' category) because I think enough has been said on these already.

The first of these is the saying that the definition of insanity is doing the same thing over and over again and expecting different results. It's often used in relation to addiction. I think this needs to be dispelled not least because no addict is insane. Addiction is not insanity (even though it can feel like it for both the addict and the friends and family of the addict). There is a logical and scientific reason that the addict keeps returning to their drug of choice; the fact that most people do not understand these reasons does not make the addict insane. Associating addiction with insanity is victim blaming; it is saying that it is the individual that is at fault and not the drug. This is nonsense. The reason a person keeps returning to their drug of choice is due partly to desperation and partly to the way the human brain works.

In many ways the human brain is like a computer. It works in certain predefined and logical ways. Everything it does has a reason if only you can understand it. If you don't understand it, it can seem to act in an entirely irrational way but this is not the case. When I write I use Microsoft Word and I always struggle when it comes to numbering the chapters and some of the paragraphs. Sometimes when I do this the numbering goes completely out of sync, the indent and borders change, the spacing between the lines changes, even sometimes the font, and this all seems to happen completely outside of any logic. However there is logic behind it, I just don't properly understand how the program works. This is what we do when we are addicted to something. In the same way that I would try the same thing (or a variation of it) again and again and again out of desperation when trying to number my chapters, so the problem drinker will return again and again to the drink as they constantly flit between what they consider to be the lesser of the two evils; life with the drink and life without it.

If you woke one day in a strange room and wanted to leave and tried the door only to find it locked would you spend the rest of your life in that room never trying to open the door again? Would you think, 20 years down the line, 'Well there's no point trying the door again, it was locked when I tried it that one time 20 years ago so logic must dictate it will still be locked now'? Would you consider someone insane if they tried that door more than once? Or do you think it would be perfectly normal to try that door again and again and again through sheer desperation? To try all different ways and means to open it? I'd think someone insane if they didn't try that door over and over and over.

To be clear here the locked room isn't an analogy for addiction, it represents a mediocre and unsatisfying life. A life where things do not feel right. A life that we want to change to make it feel right and good and enjoyable again. The addict is trapped in a life that they think is not enjoyable, not satisfying, or not as enjoyable as it could be. The addict knows instinctively that things are wrong when they are taking their drug, but they also feel that things aren't as good as they ought to be when they stop.

We've covered off previously in this book how, over time, our view of drinking changes and if we do not prepare and be on our guard we can become increasingly likely over time to start drinking again. We have also covered off how, if you quit in the wrong way, you can find yourself bouncing between two very miserable states; the state of taking the drug and the state of not taking it. Over time your perception of each state changes so you keep flitting from the one to the other. There is no insanity involved, just the working of the human body and brain.

The next platitude I want to dispel is that an addict has to hit rock bottom before they can start recovery. This is not only incorrect, it is also dangerous and contributes to the problem.

Firstly why should an addict have to hit rock bottom before looking to remedy the situation? If you had a bad cough that you weren't shaking off and you went to the doctor, what would you think if he or she said;

"Yes, this is getting quite serious. But as yet it's still just a cough. I suggest we wait for it to develop into pneumonia, then pleurisy, then when it's bordering on respiratory failure which will kill you, I'll give you some antibiotics."

Or to put it another way imagine if you were addicted to a drug that you were taking one dose of everyday at a cost of £5 that left you feeling tired and irritable all day. You have a choice of curing this addiction today or in ten years' time. If you cure yourself in ten years' time you'll be up to ten doses a day and you will have lost your family, your friends, your job, and your house, you'll have long term serious health issues and, perhaps worse than all of these things, you'll have been very very miserable for all of those ten years. That means 10 years of your life blighted and ruined.

When would you choose to cure yourself?

In fact the reason why the idea of having to hit rock bottom has become so prevalent is that addicts who have sunk very low are least able to convince themselves and others that they can control the drug or moderate. It is also the case that the lower you sink the less able you are (even with the warping of perception that happens over time) to look back on the days of their addiction with nostalgia.

All recreational drugs start off being apparently enjoyable with very little downside. Over time the enjoyment decreases and the downside increases which should make it easier to stop, but what also increases is the illusion of dependency – that we have to have the drug to cope with, or enjoy, life. You end up needing the drug just to feel normal and you feel anxious and miserable without it. You end up like a child with a smelly little comfort blanket. How will I enjoy Christmas without my little drug? How will I enjoy my holiday? How will I enjoy going out with my friends? I need my little drug with me to enjoy all of these things!

The less apparently enjoyable the drug and the more detrimental the ill-effects the more likely the addict is to be able to stop long term.

The more miserable their life with the drug is the more likely they are to be able to stick with a life without it. It is also sometimes (but not always) the case that the lower the addict sinks the less vulnerable they are to the effects of FAB and ambition. People who have lost their friends, family, home and job to drink are sometimes less inclined to then fall for the illusion that life with the drug is somehow sweeter or better.

With alcohol this aspect is exacerbated because drinking is so widespread and such a big part of so many people's lives. People search desperately for any excuse not to stop, to convince themselves that they don't have a problem and generally speaking those who have suffered the most damage from their drinking are the ones who are least likely to be able to convince themselves that they don't have a problem so pretend to themselves that they can safely drink again.

The other problem of course that this 'rock bottom' belief causes is that it makes quitting drinking shameful because it leads to the assumption that anyone who has stopped drinking must have had a serious problem with alcohol and is one of the tainted few, instead of just being someone who has taken a sensible and logical decision to cut something unpleasant out of their lives.

In fact rock bottom should have absolutely no impact on your decision to quit. I have said before and continue to say, the decision to stop drinking should not be;

'Am I alcoholic? If so stop drinking, if not continue'.

It should be;

'From a simple costs / benefit analysis, is drinking alcohol worth doing?'

To put it another way is the slightly dulled feeling you get from each drink worth the corresponding feeling of anxiety as the drink wears off, the insomnia, the lethargy, the weight gain, the arguments, the hangovers, the blackouts and the financial cost?

If the answer is 'no, it's not worth it' then the only logical thing to do is quit. The more years down the line you are the more likely you are to come to the conclusion that it's not worth carrying on, but if you fully understand the nature of alcohol even those just starting out will find it hard to justify continuing.

Some people see alcohol as a way of life, as a defining feature of their personality, a way of coping with life. It's none of those things, it's just a drug that makes you feel slightly dulled that people just happen to put into their bloodstream by drinking it instead of injecting it, smoking it, or snorting it.

The final point to make on this subject is that rock bottom for every addict is death. Other than this their rock bottom is only rock bottom so far. Unfortunately with drugs there is always another level to descend to. Why on earth should you wait for it to utterly destroy you before cutting it out of your life entirely? This is particularly the case with drugs where dependency increases over time. The best time to stop is now, it always has been and it always will be. You've already thrown away enough of your precious time and life being miserable because of a drug, why would you want to waste another single second on it?

The next phrase I want to examine is one of the most powerful tools in quitting for many people and it is the idea of taking it one day at a time. This is a very powerful tool because many people find the idea of never ever drinking again too big to comprehend. It is too powerful, too insurmountable, too much for them to hope to achieve. So they just take it one day at a time. They just concentrate on this one day, on not drinking for today, of making it to bedtime sober. They can't envisage going their whole life not drinking but they can manage a day so they just concentrate on each day as it comes.

If it is such a powerful tool for quitting why do I take issue with it? Before I go into this let me make one thing absolutely clear. This book and Alcohol Explained sets out my understanding and analysis of the alcohol trap. In them I set out how I see things, why I see them the way I do, and the tools and ideas I think are useful to quitting in the most effective way. I do not expect everyone to agree with everything I say. This is not a set menu, it is a buffet. You come, you look at what is on offer, you take what you like and you leave what you don't like the look of. My goal is not to have you, the reader, agree with everything I say. My goal is for you to finish this book a few steps, or ideally many steps, closer to your goal of living a happier, better life. If you use the 'one day at a time' doctrine to good effect then disregard what I am about to say and continue to use it.

Having now put in my disclaimer let me now explain why I take issue with this phrase. The whole purpose of the phrase is that it is based on the position that going your whole life, or even an extended period, without drinking is impossible because alcohol is a key part of your life. It creates an ongoing daily battle. If your goal is to never drink again, surely it is best to reconcile yourself with that fact? Why should you need to take one day at a time? To put it another way, remember what we covered right at the beginning of the book; that the very essence of addiction is that the addict believes that they need their drug to cope with or enjoy life. Our solution is to reeducate ourselves so that our core belief is that we do not need the drug to cope with or enjoy life, that we can live a full and happy life without our drug. Indeed that life is massively improved once the drug is removed from the equation. If we get to that stage, why on earth would we need to take one day at a time?

If you had cancer and believed you were about to die then went in for an operation to have it removed and the operation was successful would you need to take one day at time when starting out on your new, cancer free, life? You might be physically weakened by the cancer and the operation, it may takes months to fully recover, but even so you wouldn't be thinking that you can't envisage having to go through the whole of the rest of your life without cancer, so you'll just concentrate on going each day without cancer. The doctrine of taking each day at a time presupposes that a life with alcohol in it is a far sweeter life than one without alcohol in it, that you will be missing something tremendously important when you quit and that life will be significantly less exciting without it.

For me 'one day at a time' is only of use for people who still believe that there is some genuine pleasure in drinking in which case they have failed to see through the illusion. It also stops people from going through a key mental process of stopping and that is accepting that they will never drink again. Once you accept that you will never

ever drink again life becomes far simpler and far better with far less time having to be dedicated to 'recovery'.

Alcohol is a fairly pathetic little drug. It gives so little and takes so much. The only reason it has the hold over us that it does is because the vast majority of the population takes it regularly and they build up this huge world of lies and fantasy around what it is. It just makes you feel slightly dulled but because we tend to take it when we are relaxing or otherwise enjoying ourselves we start to ascribe far more credit to it than it is actually due. Then when it wears off it leaves an anxious, out of sorts feeling that gets stronger and stronger as the years go by, so that when we then take a drink and we find that it relieves that anxiety caused by the withdrawal we then again start to ascribe to it far more than it is due. The withdrawal makes life difficult and hard work, it exaggerates our usual fears and worries so that relieving the withdrawal by taking another drink fools us into thinking that alcohol is necessary for us to enjoy our lives to their full. When people are in this situation a part of them knows they are in the grip of something unnatural and unpleasant. No matter what lies they tell themselves there are a few inescapable facts that they cannot escape from; that before they started drinking they were able to cope with and enjoy their lives, that every time they wake up they feel worse for drinking, and that there are people out there who don't drink and yet live full and enjoyable lives. No one can escape from these truths but equally they cannot be parted from their drug so they do the best they can which is to paint their addiction in the most positive light. Hence the social media images glamorising drinking, the fine glassware, the expensive bottles of wine and whiskey and craft beers. The problem is that because something in the region of 90% of the population drink they all buy into this great charade which makes seeing through it even more problematic and even when you do see through it, it is very easy to keep getting sucked back in.

Taking each day at a time buys into this mirage and makes quitting a daily chore whereas accepting that you will never drink again can be extremely liberating. I don't put daily effort into my not drinking. It is now just a part of me, like the colour of my eyes. I have quit and I will never drink again. I have absolutely no interest in drinking again. I see through the nonsense and I'm happy with that. Instead of having to spend each day not drinking I've made a single decision and moved on. Trust me there are far more enjoyable and rewarding things to put your effort into. Don't take it one day at a time, make your decision, accept it, embrace it, then get on with living your life to its fullest.

The next thing I want to cover off is the generic thinking that the addict is deficient in some way and that alcohol is in some way powerful.

Admitting that you are deficient or powerless is very debasing, it is a form of surrender. It is giving up. It leads to low self-esteem and the problem is that low self-esteem contributes to problem drinking. There have been numerous studies marking this tendency but really it's just common sense. Although we do drink during the good times, it's drinking to get through the bad times where the problems really kick in. Drinking to anaesthetise problems is the crux of problem drinking in many ways. If we feel weak, damaged, different or inferior to others, these are exactly the kinds of feelings that make us want to drink more. It also provides a ready-made excuse to continue drinking; it's not my fault, I have a defect that means I can't stop drinking.

Seeing yourself as weak or seeing alcohol as powerful can in some ways be useful. It can be exactly the thing to stop you thinking that moderation is an option, after all if you are at the stage where you know alcohol is far stronger than you then you are presumably past believing in the moderation myth. Seeing yourself as battling your addiction or the substance to which you are addicted to can also be helpful as it starts us seeing the substance as an enemy rather than a friend. But the problem is this isn't accurate.

Alcohol isn't a sentient being. It doesn't have a mind and will of its own. It's not a demon that possesses us (although at times that is exactly how it feels). It's just a chemical. It holds no more power over you than a pebble or a lump of copper or pile of salt. The fact is that no drug has innate power, the only power it has is the power we cede to it. If you believe that you need something to enjoy and cope with life you will move heaven and earth to keep it in your life and it will have power over you and all the willpower in the world won't help you. But if the substance in question holds no interest for you at all it becomes an irrelevance. It holds no power over you at all.

The best analogy for addiction is a magician demonstrating his power and then using it to make you do terrible things out of fear. Imagine a magician that was real, who could kill or maim with a wave of his hand. Imagine he told you to leave your family without a word, never explaining why you left or he would maim or kill them. Would you go even though you knew it would hurt them desperately for you to go and that for the rest of their lives they would wonder why you left and believing you no longer loved them even though they were the most precious and wonderful things in your whole universe? Of course you would, you would have to.

But imagine if someone could explain to you that this magician was not magic at all and that all his tricks were just clever illusions, that he had no power or control over you at all? Well that would be very different wouldn't it? You'd be free. You could ignore him and get on with your life, knowing he was just a pathetic old man with a few clever tricks up his sleeve, tricks that could no longer leave you in awe now you understood them. There is a quote in Game of Thrones about power lying where people believe it lies, about it being just illusion. This is exactly the case. Think of the kings of ancient dynasties who held the power of life and death over hundreds of thousands of people. Those kings were just human beings, at any time their subjects could rise up and destroy them, but because everyone believed they had ultimate power, because everyone ceded power to them and did what they were told, the effect was the same.

The reality is that when we are addicted to a chemical substance our battle is not against that substance but against ourselves. Addiction comes about because our brains are only partly conscious. We tend to forget this and think of ourselves as entirely rational creatures. However we are like every other creature on the planet in that much of what we do is automated. Alcohol tricks this subconscious, automated, part of our mind. It appears to confer a benefit in that it eases anxiety and tiredness and an apathy towards life. In this way it becomes a crucial and extremely important part of our lives. But what this unconscious part of our mind is missing is that the anxiety, tiredness and inability to really enjoy life which alcohol relieves was caused by alcohol withdrawal in the first place.

In seeing addiction as a battle between us and a substance we think in terms of having to be strong enough to win a fight, we start to see it in terms of 'will power' and 'strength'. If we fail to stop we think of ourselves as 'weak'. But think of the reality. Alcohol is just an inanimate chemical. It cannot physically force you to do anything. There is one reason and one reason alone you keep drinking it and that is because a part of you wants to keep drinking it. It may be that another part of you hates it and wishes you didn't want it, but part of you must still want to drink otherwise there would be no addiction. In seeing addiction as a battle between us and a substance we draw attention away from the real issues at stake which is how our minds work and how they can become confused by the effect that drugs have on them.

Giving up alcohol isn't about power or strength or willpower. It is about understanding, knowledge and perception. It is about seeing the drug as it actually is, without all the window dressing that society adds to it. This is why alcohol is in many ways the most difficult drug to quit. How can we get to, and remain at, the stage when we see alcohol as it really is without any of the hype (and by 'hype' I mean the 'it's good for you', 'a night without a drink isn't the same', 'not drinking is so boring', 'what would Christmas / birthdays / holidays / weddings / weekends etc be without a drink?'), when nearly 90% of the population all drink and therefore want to believe in the hype and consequently have a vested interest in promoting it? As we've covered before, people are compelled to show their drinking in the most positive light possible and they do this by constantly promoting the 'hype'.

The next phrase I want to put under the spotlight is 'drinking is just borrowing happiness from tomorrow'.

One of the central frustrations of the drinker is the fact that we get alcohol into our bloodstream through our stomach (we imbibe it by drinking it, it goes into our mouths and from there into our stomach where it works its way into our digestive system before eventually ending up in our bloodstream). So if we've eaten so that our stomachs are full, it takes far longer for the alcohol to get into our bloodstream. The reason that alcohol being in our bloodstream is important is because this is when we feel the effect of it.

The problem is that alcohol is also an appetite stimulant and it also prevents us from absorbing certain key nutrients which leave us in a state of almost perpetual hunger and the lack of good quality sleep also causes us to feel additionally hungry as our body craves additional calories to give us extra energy to make up for the lack of sleep.

So alcohol makes us eat which fills us up but this also slows down the speed at which the alcohol reaches our bloodstream. Compare this to, for example, smoking where you can eat as much as you like, have a cigarette, and get the drug (in this case nicotine) into your bloodstream at the same speed as usual (as the nicotine is absorbed through the lungs, having a full or empty stomach doesn't affect it).

This is one of the central frustrations of the drinker; many of them are constantly trying to either eat or drink. As soon as they finish one drink the alcohol starts to leave their system, the corresponding stimulation that their brain has introduced to counter the depressive effects of the alcohol starts to hold sway so they start to feel anxious, bad tempered and out of sorts. So the natural tendency is to keep drinking. But the drinking also makes them feel hungry, then when they eat they become full which makes drinking harder and means it takes longer for the alcohol to reach their bloodstream.

Of course as you progress along the alcohol road you start to cotton on to this (on either a conscious or subconscious level) so you start to avoid eating when you are drinking so you can keep relieving the withdrawal caused by the previous drink. This becomes easier because the over stimulation that you experience when the depressive effects of the alcohol wears off actually decreases our appetite (as we've covered previously stimulants tend to decrease our appetite, whereas depressants tend to increase it). This is why, as people become increasingly dependent on alcohol, they tend to eat less and less. This is partly due to the ever-increasing levels of stimulation and partly due to the tendency to avoiding food so that they can experience the effect of the alcohol uninhibited by a stomach full of food.

This is also the reason for the beer-belly. Of course a beer belly isn't caused by beer, if it were it would disappear as soon as the beer had been urinated out. What it is actually caused by is drinking (which itself contains a huge amount of empty calories), then eating, then the alcohol starting to wear off leaving a feeling of anxiety. So you are forced to drink more, even though your stomach is now full of food. The alcohol then depresses the receptors which tell you how uncomfortably full you are and causes you to be hungry even though you are so full you can scarcely move, so you eat more, then drink more, then eat more etc. etc. etc. This merry-go-round usually ends when we give up and go to bed, to toss and turn all night as the alcohol wears off leaving us over stimulated and unable to sleep, and additionally uncomfortable due to the overeating. And of course overriding all of this is the fact that the accelerated heart rate makes any form of exercise increasingly unpleasant and difficult. This is an incredibly frustrating and unpleasant place to be (and is in fact the reality of Christmas drinking which I cover in more detail later on – we think of Christmas drinking as those first couple of drinks, but the vast majority of Christmas drinking isn't the first couple of drinks, it's all the rest of them, when we are feeling full up, tired and frustrated).

Where is all this pleasure that you are supposedly borrowing from the following day?

It's an incredibly unpleasant and frustrating process. So why do we do it? All for the 'pleasure' of momentarily experiencing that feeling of peace and confidence we get when we take a drink and to briefly numb the overstimulation and the exhaustion caused by the previous drinks, and return for a few moments to how we would feel all the time if we only stopped drinking for good. My point here is that it isn't pleasant while you're doing it, the most that can be said is that the first couple of drinks are enjoyable, but the rest of them aren't.

I mention a lot that the feeling of having a drink is just a lightly dulled feeling. Let me clarify this. There can be a genuine 'buzz' when we first take a drink. For regular drinkers this is primarily from numbing the tiredness and anxiety caused by the previous drinking. Even occasional or binge drinkers however can get a buzz from those first couple of drinks in the right circumstances. Don't forget your brain gives you a boost of those naturally occurring 'feel good' chemicals when you socialise. The problem is that we are also products of our society and most people find that socialising is accompanied by some form of anxiety as we worry about what people will think of us, whether we will say something stupid, and how others will perceive us. As I've covered before you get the 'feel good' boost when you are relaxed and socialising and if you aren't relaxed you won't get it.

So most people don't get the boost as soon as they start socialising because they are usually nervous to one degree or another. It takes a while for them to start to relax and as they do so the 'feel good' boost kicks in. We are all different and some people find that they relax into the evening quite quickly while for others it can take a considerable time, but in the right company everyone can get there in the end.

Alcohol, being an anaesthetic, can anaesthetise our nerves which in turn leads to the 'feel good' boost kicking in at an earlier time. This is the 'buzz' people attribute to alcohol but in fact it is not an alcohol buzz at all; it is a serotonin / endorphin buzz that you would have got anyway even if you hadn't drunk (albeit it would take a bit longer to kick in). The problem is that as the alcohol wears off it leaves an anxious, uptight feeling which needs another drink to relieve it and the additional drinks anesthetise not only the anxious feeling but also the wonderful feeling of the naturally occurring buzz that we should be enjoying. Forget drinkers at the start of the evening, look at them halfway through the evening. Where is all this happiness they are supposedly borrowing from tomorrow? Are they any more happy than non-drinkers (and I'm not referring to those non-drinkers who are miserable because they still believe all the hype about drinking and who find stopping an eternal penance, I'm talking about those who have no interest at all in drinking)? It can be hard to find these people because so many people in society drink and those who don't tend to still believe the hype and feel like they are missing out but you can always find one or two at every social occasion of any size, and looking at social occasions in countries and cultures where consuming alcohol is not the norm leaves you in no doubt.

Bearing all this in mind you can start to see how the phrase 'drinking is borrowing happiness from tomorrow' is such nonsense. When you go out with drinkers watch them. See if you don't find a marked tendency for them to be fairly lively and chatty earlier in the evening but then either no better off mood wise, or more likely far worse off, than you who are not drinking as the evening wears on (particularly after eating). The drinkers don't realise this because each drink does give them a boost but later on the 'boost' takes them from feeling anxious and annoyed to feeling slightly less anxious and annoyed. Because each drink makes them feel better than they did before they drunk it they continue to see alcohol as a friend that helps the evening. They don't appreciate that even during the course of the evening their mood is worse than had they not been drinking and of course they miss out on the 'feel good' buzz as the naturally occurring feel good high is increasingly anaesthetised.

Saying that drinking is borrowing happiness from the next day suggests that overall you end up neither winning nor losing; tomorrow may be unpleasant but you have had a doubly good night the evening before. This clearly isn't the case. You certainly do have a bad following day but you don't gain anything the night before either, in fact even during the night before the drinker is worse off than if they were not drinking.

Of course this isn't always the case. Many people go out and enjoy the whole evening whilst drinking but don't forget humans are social animals. We enjoy socialising (even for an introvert like myself, what I have found is that it is not the socialising per se that I dislike but that I need to be in company I feel comfortable with to enjoy it and the vast majority of the time I'm not in company I feel comfortable in). So often people are actually enjoying themselves despite of, and not because of, the alcohol. If you think alcohol is necessary for social occasions what do you think people in Muslim countries do? Do you think they never socialise and enjoy themselves? I know from experience that they do, but I'll tell you something they don't do, and that is get involved in the drunken bickering, arguments and violence that we in the West live with.

Obviously I have not covered off every platitude and meme out there about drinking and alcohol but I hope I have showed you that nothing should be taken for granted where alcohol is concerned and that by using a bit of common sense and applying your own logic can give you a very different picture to that which you might otherwise have. This is what you need to do if you want to quit. I am not asking you to take my word for it, or to blindly adopt my view of things, but to form your own view based on your own experience.

## 13. The Binge Drinker

I am aware that a lot of this book is centred around the regular drinker which is odd because I myself was never a regular drinker, I was always a binge drinker. I would drink heavily at weekends then abstain all week. So I think it is worth putting in a few comments about the binge drinker.

Obviously the dynamic with the binge drinker is slightly different as they don't go through life only experiencing either the withdrawal or the drinking. But there is a tendency among binge drinkers to drink more when they are drinking to drink more. Binge drinkers tend to do exactly that; binge, so they often drink just as much over the course of a week as regular drinkers, if not more.

Binge drinkers often find it harder than regular drinkers to accept that they have a problem. After all they don't drink every day, how on earth can they be addicted to it? The fact is that the only difference between the regular drinker and the binge drinker is that the binge drinker gets used to going through an entire withdrawal process before drinking again. Because they tend to drink far more on each occasion they often end up with full hangovers, the withdrawal is all mixed up with the hangover. They will wake up feeling awful and regretful and deeply concerned about their lifestyle, but after a day or two the anxiety, nausea, and hangover is gone. A day or two after that they are back to sleeping properly and a day or two after that they are back to normal, that is to say bright and confident and happy. So drinking no longer looks like a bad idea, it looks like fun and that is just in time for the weekend so off they go again.

The problem is of course that most people's weekends are Friday and Saturday night so binge drinkers will often drink Friday night and feel awful on Saturday but try to drink Saturday night as well. It's hard work to begin with and in those early years Friday drinking tends to be far more enthusiastic than Saturday drinking because the binge drinker is struggling to drink on a Saturday. But with hard work and repeated effort they soon find that their attempts to drink through their Friday night hangover on a Saturday night are rewarded. So what's the reward? The reward is the conscious and subconscious knowledge that more alcohol will remove the ill effects of the previous days drinking. In this way they go from being repulsed from drinking on a Saturday and having to work hard to drink at all, to looking forward to getting back on it on a Saturday so they can feel better.

The next stage of course is the Sunday drinking. After all, you feel rubbish when you wake up on a Saturday but very soon find that a few drinks make you feel a whole world better, so why not the same on a Sunday? The problem is that you've got work on a Monday so you don't have a day to recover, and that's where the problems really kick in. In your earlier drinking years you struggle to drink your way through a hangover, in your later years you struggle not to.

Someone messaged me once to say that he was a binge drinker and to ask why the withdrawal kicked in a few days after drinking. What he meant of course was that he didn't want to drink the day after drinking, but a few days later he did. This is the classic early stage binge drinker drinking pattern. Drink, feel awful and need to wait until you feel better before drinking again. In this way the desire to drink again didn't kick in for a few days later, which he was interpreting as the 'withdrawal'.

In terms of addiction the binge drinker can be just as addicted as anyone else, and by this I mean that they have to have alcohol to get through certain situations just like the regular drinker, but where the regular drinker cannot envisage an evening without drinking, so the binge drinker cannot envisage getting through the weekend without drinking. Incidentally I refer to binge drinkers as drinking at the weekend. This is often the case but isn't always. Some people, for example, work shifts or weekends in which case the same dynamic applies just that they may drink on whatever days they have off work.

If you drink at weekends then two days of the week you are drinking. The excess stimulants will last 1 or 2 days (possibly 3) and it is likely you are missing out on sleep for a few days after that. They then start all over again. So although they may not be suffering from the sleep deprivation and constant withdrawal in the same way that a regular drinker will, they are still a long way from feeling as good as they would if they quit. They never quite recover from the previous drink before starting the whole thing all over again. For men they will also be suffering for reduced testosterone for the majority of the time.

In many ways binge drinkers have an easier time quitting than regular drinkers, certainly from a physical perspective. The physical withdrawal aspect for them is no different to their usual post binge hangover. Where they do struggle is learning to enjoy their weekends (or days off or whatever triggers their drinking days) without alcohol, which brings us back to some of the basic tools that we can utilise to assist us in regaining control of our lives, so let's now move on to these tools for quitting. The first thing you need to do when you quit is to pick your time. For some people (myself included) this momentous occasion is dictated by circumstance and isn't really planned. You just wake up after a particularly heavy session and decide (or are told) that enough is enough. This may be your last chance before you lose your job, your marriage, your children, whatever, and the circumstances may be enough to drive you into sobriety. Others may just be feeling that their drinking needs to be cut out and are wondering how best to go about it. Still others may know they need to stop but just can't seem to manage it. So let's start off this second section of the book by providing some additional tools for sobriety, with some suggestions for how to go about stopping if you don't have it forced upon you in one form or another.

## 14. The Tools for Quitting - When to Quit

If you are someone who just seems to be repeating day 1 over and over again or if you are still drinking and considering when best to stop remember that sometimes when you hit an obstacle you need to back track a little way to allow yourself a run up.

The usual dynamic when you try to quit is that you spend your time wanting to drink and when you want to drink the tendency is to fantasise about it. When we fantasise we look only at the good part, we build it up in our minds to be far more than it is. Remember ambition and how we idolise what we don't have. So when we aren't drinking we idolise it and fantasise about it and ascribe far more benefits to it than it actually has and when we are drinking we tend not to really think about it at all. When we drink we are usually watching tv or chatting to friends or in some way distracting ourselves from the actual experience of drinking (which is a rather mediocre feeling at best). But when we are drinking we don't have that unpleasant mental background noise which is fretting over something that we want and also the low (or high) level anxiety and tiredness that is caused by all the previous drinks we've drunk. So our existence is either feeling anxious and tired and miserable and fantasising about drinking when we aren't drinking, or feeling a measure of peace and relaxation when we do drink. It is part physiological and part psychological but in both states the alcohol seems to win.

So if you are still drinking but looking to stop it can be incredibly powerful to change the dynamic for a spell. Instead of not drinking and fantasising about drinking, drink and fantasise about how things would be if you weren't drinking.

Firstly you need to give yourself a time period, with a set end at which point you will quit. The exact period is for you to choose but I would suggest not less than a week and not more than a month. It can be an actual date, or it could be at a certain event (the obvious one being when you finish this book). But whatever you decide on is set in stone and can't be changed.

Then, for that period, drink what you would usually drink knowing that you will make no attempt to stop until your deadline comes.

When you are drinking really concentrate on the reality of it without any of the usual distractions, and when you aren't drinking (i.e. when you wake up in the night after drinking, when you wake up the next day, during the day, etc) really think about how different you would be feeling if you had never taken an alcoholic drink in your life (or if you had quit several months ago).

So every time you wake up anxious in the middle of the night and can't get back to sleep, to lay there worrying about anything and everything, think about how you'd be sleeping a deep, restful sleep if you had stopped drinking. Every time you wake up feeling exhausted and miserable think about how you'd be waking up bright and positive if you'd stopped drinking. Every minute of the day when everything is hard work and effort and all you want to do is crawl away and roll up into a ball like a hedgehog under threat, think about how you'd be flying through things effortlessly if you hadn't been drinking. Think about it every time you feel fat and out of shape, when you are frustratedly over-eating fast food you really don't need because alcohol has created a false hunger.

Most importantly think about it when you finally have a drink and get your pay check for all the misery and heartache and loss of quality of life you are sacrificing. You need to drink without any of the usual hype and distractions. So if you go to the pub with friends on a Friday night and have two or three glasses of wine then when Friday night comes have the wine but just not at the pub with your friends. Drink your drinks alone at home; no tv, no music, no company. Sit alone, just you and your drink. After all, people everywhere are telling you alcohol is fun and enjoyable and makes you relaxed and happy. I'm telling you it doesn't. Who do you believe? Them or me? The answer should be neither. You need to put it to the test for yourself. You do this by drinking without the usual distractions that stop you from experiencing what the actual effect of drinking alcohol is. If you take a drug that makes you feel slightly different, but only take it when you are already relaxed and enjoying yourself, you will start to associate the drug with the good times, you will start to think it is the drug and not the situation that makes you feel good. Taking drugs is about making you feel a certain way but if you always take a drug when you are sitting down to relax at the end of the day or when you meet friends or when you are listening to music you like then how do you know if it is the drug that makes you feel good or your circumstances? There's only one way to find out; put it to the test. Separate it out and experience it as it really is.

When you sit alone and drink that first drink of the day really analyse how it makes you feel, really concentrate on that 'wonderful buzz'. This is the big moment, this is what all the fuss is about. What's so great about it? Is it such a wonderful feeling? You may feel less tired and anxious after it but that isn't a benefit of drinking because the vast majority of that tiredness and anxiety was caused by all your previous drinks. Compare it to how you'd feel if you hadn't drunk. If you had never drunk you'd feel generally positive, happy, fit, energetic and buoyant. Do you feel like that (or better than that) after that first drink? Or do you just feel slightly less tired, lethargic, and anxious than you did before that first drink? Is it wonderful feeling of euphoria or do you just feel slightly disoriented and dulled? Where is all the happiness you are borrowing from tomorrow? You need to make very sure it is there because you'll be paying just as dearly the next day as you ever do and you'll be losing years off your life span, and if the great pleasure isn't there then what on earth do you actually get out of this?

Compare how you feel after any subsequent drinks. Do you feel good? Or tired and depressed? Again compare it how you'd feel if you'd never drunk. If you were feeling angry or miserable or upset before you started do you feel less so now? Are you feeling happy and relaxed and carefree? Or just as miserable, if not more miserable, then when you started?

Compare how you feel to how you would feel if you hadn't been drinking. Think about how it's speeding up your heart rate and eroding your fitness and making you feel heavy and lethargic and weak. Think about how your brain is producing chemicals to counter the depressive effects of the alcohol and how this will ensure you wake up in the middle of the night (or at the very least sleep very badly). Think about all the empty calories you're consuming and how your liver will now have to deal with all the poison inside you. Think about any 'warming' sensation you get from the drink, about how that is a cancerous chemical burning through your living cells. But above all concentrate on exactly how it makes you feel. After all, that feeling is what you get in return for the bad sleep, the weight gain, the lethargy, and anxiety and the exhaustion. Ask yourself one very simple question: Is it worth it?

Go through this process every single time you drink.

When the last day comes and you finally get to stop drinking and you take those last few drinks, drink them alone and again really concentrate on every aspect of it. Think about the foul taste, how every mouthful is going to ruin your sleep, make you exhausted and anxious the following day, make you want to eat food you would otherwise have no desire for. Think about how any 'pleasure' is simply a slight lessening of all the anxiety and exhaustion caused by the previous drinks. Really analyse and make a firm decision whether what are you paying in terms of quality of life is really worth such a paltry return.

As soon as you finish your last drink know for a fact that you have some unpleasant times ahead. Later on we are going to cover off the changes your body needs to go through before you return to that blissful state of feeling 'normal', of no longer inflicting on yourself the constant chemical imbalance caused by alcohol. Know above all that every second that goes by is a second closer to you getting back to that wonderful feeling of being positive, well rested and resilient. Everyone is different and the time scales aren't the same for everyone. But whether it takes a day or a month, every second is taking you closer as your body and brain slowly heal themselves. Whatever unpleasantness you experience you need never experience it again.

Promise yourself that whatever happens for the rest of your life, good times or bad, that you will never ever drink again. Your new life starts now. You are no longer going to drift along because, before you know it, 20 years will have gone by, 20 years you'll never get back, and you'll have spent them puffy faced, bleary eyed, miserable, tired, overweight, riddled with anxiety, and hating yourself.

Remember that alcohol is just a chemical. The only power it holds over you is that power which you yourself give up to it. The only person that can make you take that next drink is you. It's like being in an abusive relationship, but one where you are far physically stronger than your abusive partner. You can sit there and take a battering, or you can walk away. The choice is yours and has always been yours. The only way that partner can ever hurt you again is if you yourself make a decision to let them back into your life and let them start abusing you again.

You need to go into this knowing that this is it now. There is no turning back. You are giving yourself a set period to compare life as a drinker with life as a non-drinker. At the end of that period you are going to make a firm decision about which life is better. When you have made that decision and taken that step into your new life that decision is done. It is made. There is no going back. Never question it and never waste time thinking about it. You've dragged your drinking under the spotlight, you've torn it to pieces and considered every aspect of it, you've analysed it to the fullest extent possible, you've made your decision. Know that now that process is over, it is done. If you ever in the future start to think about how nice it would be to have a drink think of this experience and how you've already made your decision about whether to drink or not so don't waste time rehashing it.

You will have good times and bad just like every other human being on the planet, just know that without drinking the good times will be better and you'll be far better equipped to deal with the bad times, however frequent or terrible they may be.

There's often a temptation when setting a date to stop to aim for a quiet period with no socialising and some people even take some time off work. On one level this seems sensible as it allows you to get some sober days under your belt and build up your experience and confidence before tackling the more difficult occasions. In the next chapter we will consider this in detail and give some thought to when the best time to stop is.

## 15. The Tools for Quitting - Taking the Bull by the Horns

Everyone has their own individual quintessential drinking experiences, the things we really can't imagine doing without a drink or can't imagine enjoying without a drink. The usual way to go about stopping drinking is to avoid these situations (at least in the early days) to avoid being tempted to drink. On one hand this makes sense. Stop for a few weeks or months and get used to having stopped. Build up your ability to resist temptation and then when your sobriety is more firmly established you can then attempt these really difficult situations. But there are a few problems with this approach.

Firstly stopping drinking is not a muscle that gets stronger as time goes on. In fact often our determination to stop wanes as time goes by. As I have covered in quite a lot of detail already in this book most of the time our determination to stop is usually at its strongest as we emerge, bleary eyed and wincing, from out most recent binge. As the days and weeks go by our determination to stop fades away.

Secondly what we need to consider is how we measure success. What is it we are actually trying to achieve when we stop drinking? That's easy right? To never take another alcoholic drink again. But is that really what we are aiming for? Surely the holy grail that all drinkers are looking for is not just to never drink again, but to be happy to never drink again. Our ideal is to do everything we used to do drinking without drinking and to enjoy it just as much, if not more, than we did when we were still drinking. In fact the two things do, to a certain extent, go hand in hand. After all, if you stop and are miserable because you feel like you are missing out on situations you used to enjoy you are far more likely to end up drinking again.

If you were a boxer and your goal was to be the best boxer of all time would you achieve this by locking yourself away and refusing to fight anyone and claim to be the world's greatest boxer because you have never been beaten? Or if you were Commander-in-Chief and fighting a war that you needed to win would you achieve your objective by avoiding conflict and by constantly moving your forces around such that they never had to give battle? If you did so you wouldn't be losing as such but you certainly wouldn't win. You'd be in some kind of limbo where you would be constantly putting off the deciding conflict. Taking this approach would be even more ridiculous if your army was growing progressively weaker over time, while your enemy's was growing increasingly stronger.

Stopping drinking is essentially about learning to live your life without alcohol. That is the criteria for success. You don't achieve that by avoiding parts of your life that you would have drunk in but by going through them not drinking. You need to learn to cope with stress, anger, loss, anxiety, joy, celebration, everything, without drinking.

The key to achieving this is to firstly understand the nature of alcohol and recognise why its attraction is largely illusion. However you then need to apply this knowledge to your own experience and to accept it not only on an academic level but also on a practical level.

You don't do this by avoiding situations you used to drink in but by facing them without a drink in your hand. When you have spent the last 20 years only ever going through a situation with a drink in your hand you start to think it will be a huge deal going through it not drinking; you can scarcely imagine how you will manage it. You go in thinking it is going to be a huge event. It never is. It's like opening a door to what you are convinced is a derelict and haunted house only to find it perfectly normal inside. It's almost an anti-climax. After all no one can physically force you to take a drink. You get offered one, you say no. If you start getting harangued about it you just say you don't fancy drinking tonight. You are in charge of your own body; you and you alone decide what goes in it and you do not need to explain that decision to anyone unless you wish to do so. If someone starts pressurising you to have a drink you just look them in the eye and say thank you but you don't want one.

Just remember nothing terrible will happen to you if you never drink another drink. But terrible things will happen to you if you do.

So how do you get through those really difficult situations without drinking? Understanding what alcohol is and what it does (and more importantly what it doesn't do) for you is obviously the main key. But there are some other tools you can use as well to ensure your success. One of the most effective of these is what I refer to as The Tipping Point.

# 16. The Tools for Quitting - The Tipping Point

For those not familiar with the phrase 'the tipping point' it means the point at which one or two smaller incidents can cause a larger, more important change. This can give us a very useful weapon in our arsenal.

Take socialising for example. A lot of what people worry about when socialising sober is what everyone will say when they ask for a soft drink. In fact these things are never as bad as you think. Winston Churchill once said:

"When you're 20 you care what everybody thinks, when you're 40 you stop caring what everyone thinks, and when you're 60 you realise no one was ever thinking about you in the first place."

I think this is particularly true of drinking. Slice and dice it how you like but there tend to be 2 types of people; those who don't really enjoy drinking to any great extent and can genuinely take it or leave it, and those for whom it is an important and crucial part of their lives. The former really have no interest in whether you are drinking or not, the latter are the ones who tend to comment on it if you aren't drinking but really their only concern is whether they can drink or not. You not drinking is really neither here nor there for them as long as their own drinking isn't affected. They may make a few comments but likely no more than if you turned up with a new hairstyle. It tends to be a short detour in the conversation which then quickly moves on to (for them at least) more interesting topics.

The point is that often the tipping point when you go out socialising is that first drink. The start of the evening is always when you are most on edge and least relaxed and after the first drinks have been handed round (be they alcoholic or non-alcoholic) things tend to calm down a bit. The conversation flows and everyone (both drinkers and non-drinkers) tend to relax into the evening. Going to your first social event after many years of drinking is not uniformly difficult throughout; the hardest part tends to be the start, particularly when the first drinks are being poured and handed around.

If you find the thought of going out all evening not drinking too difficult to contemplate then stop contemplating the whole evening. Just think about the tipping point, just think about that first drink. All you need to do is turn up and when you are asked what you are drinking order your lemonade or water or coke or orange juice or whatever it is. Have your reasons ready if anyone comments on it. This can be whatever you like but have it ready. 'I've stopped drinking', 'I'm driving', 'I've got a busy day tomorrow', 'I'm on a health kick' or (my personal favourite) 'I don't fancy drinking this evening thank you'. The conversation may dwell on this momentarily but then it will move on. Often ordering a soft drink isn't even commented on and if it is the conversation never dwells on it for long.

Bearing in mind there are people in the world living on the streets in sub-zero temperatures and people who have to live with horrific disfigurements and injuries and trauma, turning up at a social event and ordering one single soft drink should be manageable.

You can use this tool with virtually any situation. You just need to identify that 'tipping point', that key moment and just tell yourself that you just have to get through that one single moment. So if you go home and drink every evening, what is the tipping point? When you are heading home past the shops? When you get in, drop your bag down, and then think 'what now?' When your other half offers you a drink? Whatever it is identify it, isolate it, prepare for it, plan how you will get through it, run through it again and again in your mind and think that all you have to do is get past that one moment and all the rest will fall into place. Some situations may have more than one tipping point but identify them in advance and concentrate on them and mentally prepare for how you will deal with them.

Often a single action will commit you to a certain path. Concentrating on that one action that will launch you in the right direction is far more manageable than trying to think of the whole journey. If I asked you to fire a rifle at a target 800 yards away would you sit there and think about every inch that lump of lead had to travel? Or would you just point and shoot and let natural momentum do the work?

Or if you asked me directions and I told you that you had a hundred miles to travel but you take the next left and then it's a straight road all the way, the part you would need to concentrate on is taking that left or putting yourself on the right road. When you've done that all the hard work is behind you.

Of course these situations are not entirely analogous and there may still be some work to do before or after the tipping point but in fact once you're on the path often it's harder to backtrack and change course instead of just carrying on the way you're going. If you go out for the evening and when you are asked what you are drinking you order a soft drink and you then explain you aren't drinking you may face some comments but once it is done it is done. It can then be more effort to order an alcoholic drink than a soft drink the next time round. The soft drink becomes your default option and if you then wish to change you have to specifically order an alcoholic drink then explain to everyone why you've changed your mind.

If you can identify that tipping point and prepare yourself to get through it (actually visualise the entire situation in your mind and run through it several times until you are happy with it) you've done the hard work before you even turn up to the event. After that it's just a case of going through it for real and letting momentum take over and then sticking to the path you're already committed too.

When I was in the military we did drill. Most people, when you mention drill, think about square bashing (i.e. marching up and down a drill square). Moving in a 'formed body of men' doesn't really have much place in modern warfare, but there were other types of (more relevant) drill we used to do. Like weapons drill.

Loading, making a weapon ready, firing, clearing blockages, reloading, stripping, cleaning, making safe. Over and over and over and over again until you were literally doing it in your sleep. Why? So that when you are freezing cold and can't feel your hands, when you are so exhausted you can scarcely think, when you are in the pitch dark, in a panic, in the most chaotic situation you can possibly imagine, and your weapon jams, you clear the blockage and keep firing without missing a step. The more stressed you are, the more in a panic you are, the more you fall back to an automatic or subconscious or learned reaction. That is one of the purposes of the subconscious, it jumps in and takes action when our conscious mind is struggling to cope. Think of the situation you are going to go through, really imagine it, and imagine ordering a soft drink. Prepare mentally for it so when the time comes you are facing a situation you have been through a hundred times before (in your mind at least).

As I say there may be more than one tipping point in which case do your best to identify and plan for each one. When you do so really visualise yourself in that situation, use your imagination to go through the whole thing in your mind and see yourself asking for a soft drink. If you are really struggling with a situation tell yourself you will do the tipping point and the second it becomes too much you will leave. You will often find you last far longer than you think and even end up actually enjoying yourself.

Going through one of these situations very early on in your sobriety can be hugely empowering. Often we think going out on a night out without a drink is going to be a huge change but it rarely is. It's still you, out in the situation you are in, just as before. The only difference is that you are not slowly dulling your senses so you can enjoy the whole night and enjoy it without fear of making a fool of yourself. Crucially when you stop enjoying it you can just leave, you aren't forced to stay on and on and on because you have an unpleasant, anxious feeling building up in you that needs a constant supply of a drug to dampen it down.

If it's a social occasion you will usually find one of two things. Either that people don't really seem to be drinking that much or they are.

When you are drinking you are dulling your senses and your perception, and your evening revolves around the alcohol. Because your evening is focussed on the alcohol and you are not able to properly observe other people, you assume that everyone else's evening also revolves around the alcohol and that everyone is getting drunk. When you actually attend a function sober you realise that a significant number of people actually aren't drinking that much. There are a lot of people who are caught up in the hype of alcohol but actually enjoy themselves perfectly well without it and so they don't really drink that much. If this is what happens then you realise that events at which you thought it was crucial for everyone to drink alcohol at aren't actually that reliant on alcohol at all.

The other type of event of course is where people are drinking a lot. These are the times where you can really see through the nonsense about 'borrowing happiness from tomorrow' and see the reality of what alcohol does to a social occasion. You are like a spy or a scientist observing a strange newly discovered mentally deficient strain of homosapien. One of the great things about being in that situation is that 'sober is perceptive' and 'drunk is obtuse'. The non-drinker will always notice the person who has had too much to drink but the drinker will never be able to tell when someone is more sober than them. When you are sober you can always tell when someone is drunk but when you are drunk you can never tell when someone is sober. You will be sober but no one else will know it.

Even if you specifically tell people you aren't drinking it will go out of their mind soon enough. You can stand there, totally invisible, and see alcohol for what it really is. Watch out for the person crying, the near fights, and the general feeling of aggression as conversations keep taking a turn for the worse. It can be uncomfortable, not because you aren't drinking but because everyone else is. They will stand too close to you, spit when they talk, you will smell the drink on them, and their eyes will slowly glaze over, they will think they are funny when they aren't and they will repeat themselves over and over and over again. When you are in the middle of this think back to the 'borrowing happiness from tomorrow' phrase and try to spot where all this supposed happiness is.

There are two very specific practical tips to remember when you are going out for the night without drinking. The first is don't try to match people drink for drink. Remember even if you are thirsty you will only need two of three soft drinks before they start to make you feel sick. Drink if you are thirsty or specifically fancy a drink, but stop if you don't. Remember you are not drinking alcohol now. When you are drinking alcohol you need a constant supply of drinks to keep the alcohol flowing into your bloodstream, now you are free you simply have no need to keep diluting your body's salt content by continually tipping liquid down your throat.

Secondly leave whenever you feel the need to. I've found that generally speaking you can get two or three hours out of a social function (provided food is served which slows down the absorption of the alcohol) before most people really start to show the effects of the alcohol. At that stage things start to get tiresome. People start to think that they are far funnier than they are, they start repeating themselves, and they start to smell. This is usually about the time I like to reach for my coat and make a move home.

What I say about drinkers may seem very judgmental but it is an objective assessment and in my experience it is absolutely true. The purpose of these books is to give you the truth and not to reinforce the hype that society has created. For too long it is the non-drinkers who are seen as weak or incomplete or deficient in some way. They have been seen as the weak ones who have had to stop their drinking because they can't control it. In fact it takes courage and perception to start to see through the hype about alcohol, and even more so to consider cutting out something that you believe is necessary to cope with and enjoy life. What I say about drinkers is based on my observation of them. If it seems judgemental then, as ever, don't take my word for it. Go out there into the world and form your own view. Go to one of these events sober and study it and form your own opinion. See if people there are either drinking so little they clearly just haven't learnt to 'enjoy' drinking, are drinking a lot and are no happier (and often much less happy) than those who are drinking, or actually enjoying themselves despite, and not because of, the alcohol.

Remember also that you attach far more importance and relevance to your not drinking than other people. Other people are either not that interested in alcohol, in which case they really have little interest in whether you drink or not, or else they do attach a lot of importance to drinking, in which case it is their drinking and not yours that holds centre stage for them. There are a couple of incidents that happened to me that really drove this home.

To give some background I stopped drinking in February 2014. In January 2015 (so just shy of 1 year not drinking) I had to go on a business trip to Cyprus. It was the usual boozy affair, out every night making the most of the company credit card. So I just tagged along, stuck to my soft drinks, and left for bed when things started to get a bit too messy. There were only 4 of us so it was quite a small group so my not drinking came up in the conversation quite a bit. A few years after this I bumped into one of my colleagues who I was on the trip with. There was an issue with one of his customers in Cyprus so we ended up talking about the Cyprus trip. He went into the 'do you remember how much we drunk this night' and 'do you remember how hammered we got that night' conversation about how drunk we got. I just smiled and nodded; he'd totally forgotten that I hadn't been drinking, he just assumed that I'd been right there drinking along with him.

A similar incident happened after myself and my family went away to Tenerife with three other families during October half term. We dined together each evening and needless to say I was on the soft drinks. A year or two after this we were out for the evening and two of the couples we were on holiday with were there. Needless to say I wasn't drinking and one of them asked me if I minded going out not drinking. I said I was fine with it and explained that I was well used to it by now as I hadn't drunk for some time. She was surprised and said 'But you were drinking in Tenerife?'

What these two incidents highlighted to me was the difference in importance I attached to my not drinking compared to other people. For me going on a business trip and an all-inclusive holiday without drinking was a big thing but for others it clearly wasn't to such an extent that they either had forgotten about it or that it hadn't really registered in the first place.

We tend to think that people push drinks on us because they are obsessed with drinking and this may be the case for many people but not necessarily for all. For some people it is just trying to be hospitable (however misguided this may be) in the same way if you went for dinner or canapés and didn't eat anything they would keep asking you if you wanted anything to eat, or if there is a buffet no one likes to be the one to start on it so the host or hostess has to go round several times trying to get people to tuck in. Offering food to people isn't considered to be rude or inconsiderate, but if the person being offered it had an eating disorder, or were struggling with a diet, then they might consider it so.

Drinkers drink because they enjoy (or believe they enjoy) drinking. Over time it becomes an increasingly large and important part of our lives. We tend to favour events that allow us to drink and we tend to socialise with other people to drink heavily but alcohol isn't necessarily a big part of all other people's lives.

Think back over your own life and how you have reacted to people who were not drinking in social situations. Did it make any real impact on you? Did you attach any relevance to it at all? Do you even remember? I don't think I have ever been to a large social event where at least one other person wasn't drinking but it was only after I had stopped that I even noticed. I can remember a few times noticing people who weren't drinking but that was only when I wasn't drinking myself and was glad to see them. There tends to be a bond between non-drinkers particularly when the evening draws on and the alcohol started to take effect such that talking to the drinkers became more and more painful, so you usually end up talking to people who are not drinking. But I cannot remember a single time when I was drinking and a person's non-drinking stuck out in my mind. I think in my earlier drinking years it wouldn't have bothered me one way or another, in my mid-drinking years I wouldn't have cared as long as I had enough to drink, and in my later years I probably would have envied them and / or wouldn't have remembered the next day anyway.

We tend to feel very self-conscious about our not drinking but I think we need to bear in mind that it often takes on a far greater significance to us than it does for other people. When you are drunk your intoxication is very noticeable but when you are sober your sobriety can remain hidden. No one ever says after a big night out 'Wow do you remember X, s/he was so sober!'. We notice people who are more intoxicated than us but never people who are more sober than us. In this way the sober people hold the upper hand at social occasions because it is they who see the most and retain the most dignity.

Obviously the ideal situation for socialising is to go to social occasions where no alcohol is served. This is becoming increasingly more common as alcohol and drinking is increasingly seen in its true light instead of through the warping effects of the hype that it hides under but there is still a long way to go.

In the next chapter we are going to look at the all-important cravings. I deal with them in some detail in Alcohol Explained but they are such a major part of addiction that I think it is worth going over them again, developing some new concepts and explaining some of those covered previously but in a different way.

# 17. The Tools for Quitting - Cravings

Let's start off this subject by going over again what a 'craving' is. It is you, fantasising about how nice it would be to have a drink. It is a conscious thought process that you are going through. Above all it is FANTASY, it is not REALITY. It is a highly romanticised, utterly distorted, fiction. A craving is simply thinking about only the good parts of something and exaggerating those good parts shamelessly. When you find yourself thinking about drinking don't FANTASISE about it. Just think about the reality. Think about the actual reality of what would happen if you had a drink. What is that reality?

The first thing you would have if you took a drink would be the unpleasant taste, the taste of empty calories thinly disguising the taste of a substance so toxic it is used as a disinfectant because it kills the living cells that it comes into contact with. Secondly, at the very second you swallowed your first mouthful, you'd have a feeling of bitter disappointment that you'd failed once again to stop. You may try to tuck that feeling away and concentrate on your socialising or your tv or whatever it is you are doing while you are drinking but you will never be able to completely ignore it. It will be there hanging over your head like a cloud full of acid rain. Thirdly you'll have a slightly dull feeling as the alcohol takes hold. Then you'll have a nervous, anxious feeling as it wore off. Then you'll face a simple decision. Either have another drink to get rid of that unpleasant, anxious feeling caused by the first drink and end up increasingly intoxicated, or suffer this unpleasant feeling for several hours. Either way you'll end up with a sleepless night of anxiety, then a following day of anxiety, exhaustion, and guilt; a day spent agonising about whether to have another drink to take the edge off the anxiety, exhaustion and guilt caused by yesterday's drinking. And so it would go on, either forever or until you made the effort to break the cycle all over again.

That's the stark reality of taking a drink. Of course this isn't what you are thinking when you are craving. When you are craving you are thinking how wonderful it would be to have a drink, how strong and confident and happy you'll feel, how you'll be the rebel, the maverick, the tough or sophisticated drinker, you'll fill your mind with all the utterly ludicrous and false drinking icons and images that we use to paper over the ugly reality of our drinking. This is what craving is. It is allowing yourself to dwell on the idea and not the reality of taking that drink.

The issue of craving however is further confused by the working of the subconscious. I deal with this topic in Alcohol Explained so will not go over it again here other than to say that the subconscious is that part of our brain which automates decision making. Often, what we think of as a conscious decision is in fact a subconscious one. To give an example if you have an argument with your partner and storm out of the house, walk the streets, then decide you couldn't care less and just head to a pub or off-licence, your analysis might be that it was while walking the streets in a rage that you decided to drink. In fact the decision to drink was made by your subconscious right back when the argument was going on; the storming out and walking the streets thinking was what I call 'the search for excuses'. The subconscious made the decision to drink, your conscious mind knows that it's an irrational decision, so to reconcile this you spend some time searching for excuses to justify the decision.

You should be able to recognise this 'search for excuses' thought process when it happens because what is going on is not a rational and calm weighing up of the pros and cons of taking a drink, it is a quick mental jump from one idea to the next, and focussing on any excuse, no matter how superficial or irrational, to take a drink, and disregarding immediately anything that goes against the decision. Often it involves laying the blame elsewhere. If we are making a conscious decision we slowly and calmly weigh up each of the pros and cons, the for and against, we think about them all, and add them together to see how they balance out and on the basis of that we make our decision. However when the decision has been made by the subconscious and we are just trying to justify it we quickly disregard anything that goes against the decision and we just make a quick list of anything that goes for the decision. If we find anything even remotely substantial that supports the decision we focus in on it and try not to think about anything that might undermine it. As soon as we have a quorum we quickly act on it before rational thinking can undermine it. The act is almost done in a panic. It is the exact opposite of a rational weighing of all the relevant factors hence my referring to it as 'the search for excuses'.

In fact we can delve even deeper into this thought process to shed even more light on it. The human brain cannot think of an infinite number of things at the same time. The current general consensus is that the human brain can think of only seven things simultaneously. If you then think of an eighth thing one of those original seven things drops away. How accurate this is I don't know, personally I feel that three is my absolute upper limit, and that is on a good day, but whatever the actual number is, it is clear that there are a finite number of things we can think about at any one time.

When we are agonising over whether to take a drink or not there are tens if not hundreds of factors in play. We believe we want it, we cannot enjoy whatever situation we are in without it, we cannot cope with life without it, it makes us feel young and carefree again, we are miserable without it, we have vowed we won't take another drink, we know from personal experience how miserable our lives are when we drink, we know it makes us tired, lethargic, bad tempered, it stops us sleeping, we are afraid to drink it, and we are afraid not to drink it, we worry about the cost in terms of finance, in terms of the strain it puts on personal relationships with our friends, family and colleagues, in respect of our job, and our house, our self-respect, the way it changes us, the way we have to have another drink when we take that first one, but am I an alcoholic or aren't I?

Above I've come up with over 20 different considerations to take into account when thinking about whether to take that drink. In reality there will be hundreds, some generic, some deeply personal to the individual. But remember you can only actively think of a small number of things at one time. If you're thinking that you're miserable without drinking, that you don't care about tomorrow you just want to enjoy a drink now, that it makes you feel young and carefree, that you can't cope with life without drinking, that other people seem able to take it or leave it, that logically if you can stop for long periods you should be able to just take one or two, that life is getting you down and you just want a bit of relief, and everyone seems to say a little of what you fancy does you good, you have already filled your brain up with everything you can think about at one time (and possibly a bit more). There is no room now for any of the reasons not to drink. You base your decision on the information you can consider at any one time, and all the points you have in your mind are all pro drinking so you reach out and grab a drink and drink it.

This is again a part of that emotive, panicky thinking that comes before giving into a craving. Again calm and rational thought is the order of the day. Keep calm and focus on the reality. Recognise it when it comes. Panicked thinking and searching for excuses to drink (i.e. reasons to drink) instead of calmly assessing the situation are both symptoms of craving and being close to caving in. We British are often criticised for 'the stiff upper lip' and our hiding our emotions but there is much to be said for calm, rational thought instead of giving into emotion. Letting emotions take over is fine if we want to communicate how we feel to other people, but if we actually want to solve our problems instead of flapping around squawking about them, then a calm, stoic approach is the order of the day.

It is worth remembering that craving starts when you think about the reality of having a drink, which is why certainty can be key in stopping you craving at all. If you are certain you are never going to drink again then you won't crave because your brain simply doesn't go down the path of 'I could have a drink now, what would it be like if I did?' which is the thought process that leads to craving. As soon as you allow this first thought into your head (the 'should I or shouldn't I' thought) you entertain the actual reality of taking a drink. So the next logical step in this process is to think about what it would be like to have that drink. The natural tendency is to fantasise and idolise what it would be like to have that drink (after all, at this moment we have stopped drinking so it is something we don't have but we are starting to think we might like to have it, so 'ambition' kicks in and we start to fantasise about it).

So in fact we get two chances to defeat any craving. Certainty stops it from starting in the first place and a good grounding in reality stops it from moving from the 'should I or shouldn't I' phase to the idolising phase. It's this latter phase where we really torture ourselves and is what most people think of as craving.

This is why so many people quit these days without craving. There is so much good 'quitlit' out there and alcohol has so little going for it when we strip away all the hype, lots of people can get to the stage where they see alcohol in its true light. The reality, once seen, is difficult to un-see. So they are happy to not drink again and / or can't forget the reality of drinking and / or are absolutely certain that they will never drink again and so they don't crave a drink.

When we dealt with ambition I explained how your concept of something you don't have is very different to your concept of something that you do have. I also explained how this created one of the central miseries of the addict; that they pine for something that isn't real, something that they have created a whole fantasy about and that they want this highly fantasised version of the drug and not the reality. When they return to their drug they are stuck with the reality and not the fantasy which of course never existed in the first place. This same result happens on a quicker scale when you give into a craving.

When you are going through the search for excuses (in other words you are desperately looking for any flimsy excuse to drink rather than sensibly weighing up the pros and cons) and when you fill your mind with seven (or however many) reasons to drink such there is no room for considering any reasons not to drink, you then make a quick and panicked decision to drink and you grab a drink and drink it.

The problem is that when you've taken the drink you then have no reason to dwell on all the things in favour of taking that drink, they are flimsy and quite pathetic anyway so now you have no reason to search for excuses and the panic is at an end. As such these flimsy reasons to drink just evaporate like the ethereal nonsense they are. You then naturally return to the reality which is 'What on earth have I just done?' Now that you have a drink in your hand (and possibly even one or two inside you) the panicked, warped thinking created by the craving is gone and the truth returns. Any drinker knows on a rational appraisal that they are a fool to drink (even without the analysis in Alcohol Explained and Alcohol Explained 2 every drinker knows that they used to be able to enjoy life without a drink when they were younger and that alcohol makes them feel unpleasant the next day). The longer you have been drinking for the more the downside of drinking becomes apparent. Most people who get to the stage of wanting to quit have seen a lot of the downside. So now you can think clearly again all these downsides flood back into your mind. So you find yourself sat there wondering what on earth you are playing at. Again you are now stuck with the reality and it's an ugly reality.

This isn't insanity, this is just your brain working as it is designed to work and being tricked by the effects of a drug. Your brain is an amazing thing but the effects of drugs trick and confuse it and addiction is the result. But the great beauty of it is that all these processes that together combine to make up addiction can be overridden by conscious thought. This is why when you are craving you can be desperate for that first drink and agonise over it but the second it finally passes your lips you wish you'd never taken it. It may feel like insanity but it most certainly is not.

In the next chapter we are going to be following along the logical progression of what happens when you decided to quit but then give in to a craving beyond the initial drink or two. After all I keep saying that you need to keep reality in mind to defeat cravings so let's look at the reality of what happens when you give in to that craving, rather than negate it.

# 18. The Tools for Quitting - The Worst Drink You'll Ever Drink

As we've covered previously we get the best 'buzz' from alcohol when it is relieving symptoms that it has previously caused. To recap briefly the brain contains a huge store of naturally occurring hormones and drugs (like adrenaline) which it releases at exactly the right time and exactly the right quantities to keep us functioning at our optimal level. It is a very delicate balance and when it is working properly we feel resilient and positive. Alcohol is a chemical depressant which upsets this delicate balance so the brain seeks to counter the depressant effects of the alcohol by releasing its own naturally occurring stimulants. The alcohol is then processed and removed from our bodies leaving just the stimulants behind. This leaves us feeling anxious, nervous and even out and out depressed (depending on the severity of the withdrawal). When we then drink more alcohol this depresses excess stimulants leaving us feeling more relaxed and feeling far more resilient than before we had a drink. However this feeling of relaxation and resilience is only the feeling of returning to how we would have felt had we never had that first drink in the first place. Drinking also leaves us tired and lethargic and, again, a drink will anaesthetise these feelings.

If you get through this withdrawal (I go through the physiological processes of quitting in a later chapter, including how you can expect to feel at the different stages and provide a rough timeline) and catch up on good quality sleep there is none of this withdrawal and tiredness to relieve. A drink, at this time more than any other, will leave you feeling slightly dulled and unable to marshal your thoughts effectively and this is about the sum total of its effect. It isn't a particularly pleasant feeling. In this way whenever you have a drink after a period of abstinence it never gives the boost or high that you are actually fantasising about in the first place because there are no excess stimulants for the alcohol to counter. Your unconscious brain won't know this of course, all it knows is that alcohol makes you feel far happier. It doesn't factor in that the 'happiness' is just relieving a chemical 'unhappiness' caused by the previous drinking. It's like a memory foam mattress (a mattress that, when you lie on it, gives under the weight of your body to provide even support for your whole body – supposedly). Imagine the level of the mattress represents how you feel. Flat is normal, raised is overly chemically depressed, and an indent or dip is overly chemically stimulated. Alcohol is a block that you put on the mattress. At first it creates an increased level (which means you feel the depressive chemical effects of the alcohol) but over time the mattress dips under the weight of the block. Pretty soon there is a block shaped hole in the mattress which the block of alcohol fits perfectly in. Take the block away and the level drops dramatically (which means you feel overly chemically stimulated, i.e. nervous, anxious and even shaky). Pop the block back in place and hey presto, you get rid of the dip and all it represents and you are left feeling confident, resilient and in fairly good spirits.

Using this analogy it is essential that you appreciate that neither a dip nor a raise is a good thing. The dip leaves you anxious, the raise leaves you dulled and confused. Putting the block back in place is only pleasurable if there is a block shaped hole to put it in. No hole, no pleasure. This is how alcohol works so if you've stopped drinking for some small period of time such that you are through the physical withdrawal there is a chemical reason why the drink won't do what you think and hope it will do. This is aside from all the psychological factors at play that mean that the idea of the drink won't measure up to the reality.

Of course this whole process is confused by the fact that the craving cycle is unpleasant in and of itself; it is in effect the torture that any addict goes through which keeps driving them back to their drug of choice. In taking a drink you do end the mental torture of the 'should I or shouldn't I' so the addict often does feel far better when they finally give in and take the drug, but that's only the pleasure of ending the mental panic and conflict and that could just as easily have been ended by calm and rational thought.

The process is further confused because, as covered earlier in the book, when human beings are happy and relaxed and socialising their brain releases serotonin and endorphins which are the feel good, naturally occurring drugs. If you are craving at a social occasion you won't be relaxed and happy, you will be uptight and miserable, so in taking a drink you not only end the unpleasant mental process of craving but you also allow the serotonin and endorphins to flow. The difference a drink makes in this situation is between misery and panic and joy and happiness. But again you could have got to the same destination via a completely different (alcohol free) route. Certainty and / or calm and rational thought could have done exactly the same without recourse to drinking. In fact often you won't get the dopamine high anyway unless you use certainty and rational thought in any event. Let me explain.

If you are at a social function and are craving a drink you will be miserable. You will be idolising alcohol and thinking how much happier you would be if you took a drink. The problem is that if you take a drink you probably won't be happy and relaxed anyway. You may have removed the mental torture but now you will feel guilty and weak. You aren't going to get a serotonin and endorphin high if you are sat there miserable because you've failed to stop drinking once again. You may try to ignore this aspect but it will be there hanging over you. This is another reason why, after a certain stage, the drinker is worse off whether they drink or not. They are miserable if they drink and miserable if they don't, either way they miss out on the wonderful natural buzz.

Remember also what we covered off about emotion, about how one drink will relieve slightly a negative emotion but as we get increasingly intoxicated the emotion spirals out of control. If your drinking is triggered by anger or upset or any other kind of negative emotion not only will the relief be extremely limited but you will end up far more angry or upset than you were before you gave in to your craving. Also if drinking makes you feel guilty and weak, then the more you drink the more guilty and weak and generally miserable you will feel.

For all these reasons if you have stopped for a bit and are craving a drink and you take one it never does what you think it will; the reality of drinking always falls far short of the idea of drinking. Often we think that this is because the drink we took wasn't strong enough or was too small so we take another. This is one of the reasons why when people think they will allow themselves just one drink they will most certainly end up taking more than one. A part of you expected that drink to make you feel great and relaxed and euphoric but it didn't, so you take another. And another. And another. The problem is the mismatch between the reality of drinking and the idea of it. It isn't the idolised fantasy we've built it up to be.

There is also the fact that as one drink wears off it leaves an empty insecure feeling and you need another drink to relieve that feeling.

The knock-on effect of this is that as soon as we've taken one drink and are overwhelmed with a feeling of failure and misery. We then try to anesthetise that feeling by drinking more and more. This is why so often when we fall off the wagon we fall hard. The next day we then wake up feeling worse than ever but now we do have the chemical mental imbalance caused by the alcohol so the next day we have even more reason to drink than we did the night before. In many ways this is the most pitiful part of it. We get the hangover and all the anxiety and self-disgust and misery the next day, but we didn't actually get the relief we were after in the first place. We pay the full price of admission without actually enjoying the show. But the next day we do get the withdrawal because we drank the day before so then when we take a drink we're off and away. And so off we go again round and round on the merry-go-round of misery that we were so desperate to escape from in the first place.

This is a huge point to keep in mind. When you have those crucial first few days and weeks of sobriety under your belt alcohol will do even less for you than it did before and will hit you with all the misery of drinking far harder than when you were drinking. This is the reality of drinking that you need to keep firmly lodged in your mind.

Just as you need to look at drinking, other drinkers, and stopping drinking in a whole new and honest way, so do you also need to start looking at yourself in a whole new way. This requires quite a large change, it requires you to change your self-image.

## 19. The Tools for Quitting - Self-Image

Self-image is a mental picture we have of ourselves. It is very resistant to change and determines how we act and react and how we deal with difficult and challenging situations. It is made up in part of a long lasting and stable set of memories. There are various studies to show that our self-image is self-perpetuating, in other words if we see ourselves in a certain way then we act in accordance with that and therefore reinforce our beliefs about ourselves.

If you are someone who has been drinking regularly for several years or decades then being a drinker will be an integral part of your self-image. Part of your self-image will be that you are someone who reaches for a drink in certain situations, good and bad. If you think for example about losing your partner, children, house, job etc. you will immediately see yourself taking a drink to deal with that situation.

The problem is of course that when many people try to stop drinking they just do it by cutting out the drink. But just deciding to quit drinking is not enough to stop us, because our self-image remains unchanged, and our self-image is that of a drinker, someone who reaches for a drink in good times and bad.

Our self-image is a mix of many different things; our nationality, our religion, our approach to life, our sense of humour, our outlook, our family, our friends, our taste in music. Drinking can touch many of these things. Take me for example. I am an Englishman and the English culture is very much tied up with drinking, from the harsh realities of city streets being awash with drunken violence on Friday and Saturday nights, to the romanticised side such a quaint pubs and stirrup cups. I previously served in the British Army whose history is inextricably linked with hard drinking. For years I saw drinking as my shield against the world, as long as I had a drink in my hand I could survey the world calmly and with humour. All my family and friends drink. Drinking was an essential part of who I am.

Some people, when they stop drinking, do manage to change their self-image and start to see themselves as a non-drinker, however many (even those who may have stopped for many years) haven't changed this self-image. Self-image isn't just made up of our view of ourselves based on our own experiences, it is also made up of those people that we look up to and aspire to be like. Not just famous people like our heroes and heroines, but also our friends and family, even colleagues and acquaintances.

I grew up near Wimbledon in the 1980's, legends of Oliver Reed's antics were regularly told (and still are). I grew up reading Bulldog Drummond, James Bond, and Richard Sharpe. My close family all drank, so did my friends. My self-image was formed around this background and in good times and bad drinks were poured and all the good and bad that life threw up was taken with a drink. Every time something happened, good or bad, I would think about dealing with it by taking a drink. Later in life I found great pleasure in watching WC Fields, Charlie Harper, and Homer Simpson. My self-image was self-perpetuating because I would be most interested in the hard drinkers and the drunks, I would seek them out and watch them, and they would become my role model, my justification if you like for my heavy drinking. I would see myself in their image, not in reality. I was not a pathetic, overweight, physically weak addict, I was the loveable rogue, the tough hardened drinker.

Self-image not only causes us to act in a certain way, it also provides a way to justify how we act. Do you see members of **ISIS** who torture helpless prisoners to death as scum who need to be wiped off the face of the earth? Or brave and strong individuals taking a stand against an insane world that is spiralling into greater and greater degradation?

How do you think they see themselves?

Do you see yourself as a drinker? Or a non-drinker?

If you are still drinking do you see yourself as someone who is addicted to a drug that makes you fat and weak and lazy and as emotionally unstable as a spoilt toddler? Or do you still see yourself as the tough guy, or the sophisticated lady, as the life and soul of the party?

Changing your self-image is hard, and it isn't just a case of realising that how you see yourself as a drinker is absolute nonsense, you also need to replace it with something else.

I was always someone who dismissed personal stories about people giving up drink. I always said if someone has managed to stop drinking why should that stop me? Their situation is different to mine, and if it wasn't I'd have no reason to read their book anyway, as I'd already have lived it! But of course, why these books are so powerful is that they provide us with examples of people who have stopped drinking and deal with life without drink, they provide us with someone we can emulate or even look up to who deal with life on its own terms, without having to have a drink in their hand.

This is another of the reasons that we need to change our view of 'recovery' if we want to successfully quit drinking, and when I say successfully I mean to cut out drinking and live a full and happy life instead of having to go the whole rest of our lives 'working on our recovery'. One of the problems with the stereotypical idea of quitting drinking is that those who quit have sunk low and can never really expect to be happy again, they spend their lives resisting temptation, taking one day at a time, staying close to whatever programme they are working, and having to always be on their guard. They spend the whole rest of their lives making a very conscious effort to not drink and relapse is common and even expected. If you have spent years building the self-image of a drinker and then quit drinking, often the most obvious alternative self-image to adopt is that of the stereotypical 'recovering alcoholic' but it is simply not helpful. You may no longer see yourself as someone who reaches for a drink when something terrible happens, but you will most likely end up seeing yourself as someone who sits there miserable and afraid and fighting cravings and having to work a programme all the time to remain sober. I am not saying this is a conscious choice, mostly we are unaware of our self-image, of how it is created and its effect on us. But like everything else once we are consciously aware of it we can stop ceding control of it to our subconscious mind, and we can control it in our conscious mind, which gives us absolute power over it. That is what much of my method is about.

Start seeing yourself as exactly what you are; someone who has stopped poisoning themselves with an addictive drug, a drug that has made you weaker (mentally and physically), fatter, unpleasant and unable to deal with even the most benign of upsets. As a consequence of stopping you are stronger (mentally and physically), fitter and better able to deal with whatever life throws at you. Start analysing your drinking role models. Are they pure fiction anyway (like James Bond)? Or even if they are real people do you really believe they were enjoying every minute of their drinking lives, or do you think they were going through the same nightmare you were when you were drinking? In fact, when you think about it, aren't they in exactly the same category as those so-called 'normal' drinkers that we no longer envy?

Drinkers often think of themselves as weak and / or stupid. This may certainly seem to be the case at first glance (after all tipping a cancerous poison down your neck on a regular basis just to rectify the effects of the previous dose isn't the most sensible thing to do) and usually if we are forced to do something we don't want to do this is seen as weakness. But we've already covered off how addiction isn't weakness, it's the brain becoming confused by the effects of the drug. If you think you are weak and stupid stop for a moment and ask yourself if you really are weak and stupid in other areas of your life or if it is just where alcohol is concerned? If it is just where the drug is concerned then surely this would suggest that it is the drug, and not you, that is the problem.

Although anyone can become addicted to alcohol I think there are some personality traits that make it more likely. Drinking a lot and drinking earlier in the day, or later into the night, than anyone else shows that you are a risk taker, someone who is independent and prepared to play by their own rules and not follow the herd. Someone with a bit of strength of character. I also think imagination plays a big part. The craving process is entirely reliant on your imagination, you are imagining how wonderful it would be to drink. The more imaginative you are the more torturous the craving will be. Physical fitness and strength also plays a part. It is a fact that the physically stronger you are the more alcohol you can handle. Also fitter people tend to be slimmer and their metabolism works faster so the alcohol is going to hit their bloodstream quicker which means the alcohol is going to be more addictive for them. Don't forget that the 'withdrawal' is the brain countering the poisonous effects of the alcohol. The more effective your body is at countering the poisons the more pronounced the withdrawal.

A lot of heavy drinkers, when they stop and actually think about it, realise that they aren't weak and stupid at all. On the contrary they tend to be stronger, more imaginative, independent risk takers. Stop for a minute and appraise yourself as objectively as you can. You may well find that you are very far from weak and stupid and in fact quite the opposite is the case. If this is the situation then why on earth should your new self-image be someone who is weak and different and in some way broken? If the only thing that has made you feel this way is the alcohol and the alcohol is about to be removed from your life once and for all then your new self-image should be based on all your strong traits with no weakness or stupidity involved.

See through the hype and lies associated with quitting drinking. If you identify with any of the personality types I mention above then see how well they lend themselves to sobriety. Nearly 90% of the population drink so if you want to quit you need to be independent, individual, able to act apart from the herd mentality. You need good imagination and intelligence to see through the nonsense and hype about drinking, drinkers, quitting and recovery. You are going to be fitter and stronger than your peers. You aren't stupid because you've used common sense and intelligence to see through the nonsense and you've shown your independence and strength of character in going against the ignorant herd and moved forward in your own way. You are going to actually deal with problems instead of anaesthetising them and if you need to escape you'll use exercise, books, films, friends, whatever you decide you use to deal with the bad times. This is you. This is your new self-image. Get used to thinking about yourself in these terms; independent, resilient, strong and energetic.

## 20. The Tools for Quitting - The Key Drinking Occasions

When you quit drinking you need to prepare in advance for any occasion you think is going to be a challenge. There's no point just turning up and keeping your fingers crossed, in the early days at least you need to run through the occasion in your mind before you get there so you are prepared and ready. In the same way that you need to start seeing drinking, drinkers, recovery and yourself in a different (and frankly more realistic) way, so you also need to see those occasions that you always believed you would never be able to go through not drinking in a new light.

When you identify these situations take a three-stage approach to dealing with them. Firstly you need to identify how you have idolised drinking in that situation and how much of that image is false. Secondly you need to identify the true pleasure in the event (after all if the only pleasure in the event is the drinking then you may as well save yourself the effort of attending and just stay at home and drink). Thirdly and finally you need to recognise how in reality alcohol will detract from the inherent pleasure in the event in question.

We are all different and although the chemical, physiological and psychological factors that make up our drinking are all very similar we all have different lives and will have different situations that we consider will be problematic. It is not possible for me to predict and cover off every situation every reader will encounter and strip it of the alcohol-soaked hype, but what I can do is give you a few of my own definitive drinking situations and show you how I now view them. These are situations that, during my drinking years, I could never have believed I could go through, let alone enjoy, without drinking. I can show you how I used to see them and how I see them now. This will hopefully give you the tools which you can translate into whichever situations you think you may need to do a bit of preparation for.

One of the most obvious ones, and I think this is true for many people, is going on holiday. When I go on holiday with my family we always go all inclusive (meaning all the food and drinks are included) so there is as much alcohol as you could want all included in the price.

This is how I used to see holidays when I was drinking: they are a time to drink uninhibited, in fact not just the holiday but the travelling as well. I used to find flying stressful, all the panic to get there, lugging suitcases around then going from hectic to bored as you wait impatiently and with increasing irritation in the crowded airport to board (a phrase that was used a lot in the British Army always used to spring to mind; 'hurry up and wait'). Then when you do finally board the plane you are stuck in horribly cramped conditions desperately waiting to get off. Then finally landing, feeling uncomfortable, tired and restless, then more waiting to get off and get through passport control, waiting for the luggage, then more lugging suitcases and hot uncomfortable coaches or taxis. The only thing that made the journey even remotely enjoyable was having a few drinks at the airport, a few more on the plane, then finally arriving to hit the bar and recuperate from the horrible journey with a few liveners.

Then the actual holiday. I would imagine waking up probably a bit hungover but who cares? A spot of breakfast, half an hour or so for that to go down, then it was perfectly acceptable to get a cold beer at the bar and lie around slowly sipping it, with a book or just relaxing and chatting. Long lazy mornings, long lazy afternoons, drinking, chatting, snoozing, reading, relaxing. Then later in the afternoon up for a shower and to dress for dinner, a nice cocktail or two with dinner, then sitting out for the evening, enjoying the warmth and the view with a drink in hand.

There may be a few days of sight-seeing, of exploring exotic, ancient cities, following meandering alleyways and going into local bars to drink ice cold drinks.

In all honesty how could anyone go on holiday, not drink, and expect to have even half as good a time as if they were drinking?

This is how I see holidays now:

Firstly it came as a huge surprise to me to find that I don't actually hate flying. We leave nice and early for the airport so it's not actually stressful getting there. Suitcases have wheels these days, so getting them from point A to point B is virtually effortless. We drop our bags off, go through security, find somewhere nice to eat, and after a relaxed meal it's usually about time to head to the gate for boarding. Then it's a few hours on a plane, which I actually don't mind at all now. I always feel like I never get enough time to just sit and read or write, which is exactly what I get when I'm on a plane (part of this book was written on a flight). When we land I feel happy, excited and ready to go. I don't feel restless or groggy or irritated. I'm bright, energetic and excited. I enjoy the coach or taxi journey, sitting there looking out the window. Even the journey back home is much the same. It's nice to be getting back and settling back into the normal routine. We usually plan to have a takeaway (takeout) when we've got home and unpacked which is something to look forward to. So why is there this huge change?

This is one of the little aspects of not drinking that never occurred to me to expect. You expect to wake up without a hangover, you expect to feel better and perhaps to lose some weight, but no one ever says 'flying is so much less stressful'. I really wasn't expecting it, after all flying is a grind whether you're drinking or not isn't it? Turns out, for me at least, that it isn't!

I was never a regular drinker, I was a binge drinker, but for me my holidays started the moment I left work so whenever I was flying I was drinking the day before the flight. So whenever I flew I had a night's drinking behind me. It made things look irritating, the queues, the crowds, the people. It made me restless which made waiting at the airport and sitting on the plane very uncomfortable and made time pass a lot more slowly. It accelerated my heart which made moving suitcases a grind instead of a breeze and of course I would drink at the airport and on the plane, so by the time I got off I would be half hungover; hot, restless, tired and irritable. I have none of those things now and it only dawned on me several years after quitting drinking just how much better travelling is when you are sober. So there's another unexpected benefit from quitting drinking; stress free flying!

As for the actual holiday, is the idyllic description I gave above an accurate representation of a drinking holiday? Clearly not, and as ever it is the idea and not the reality that is attractive. So for example the description I give above misses out the waking up in the middle of the night feeling tired but being unable to sleep. It also misses out the waking up feeling exhausted and anxious. Also missing is the feeling of lethargy and effort it takes to get up and move around. The frustrated uncomfortable feeling of constantly overeating. The feeling of being overweight and out of shape. The regular arguments and bickering.

Let's now move to the second stage of our three-stage approach and see what pleasure there is in holidays without alcohol, or what you gain from being on holiday not drinking. No hangovers obviously. Waking up rested and fresh and excited to start the day is an obvious one. But what is less obvious is just feeling good all day. You already feel well rested and positive and happy, you don't need a drink to feel that way. You can sit, and chat, and read, and snooze (just as if you were drinking). But you can also get up and go for a walk, or a run, or play with the kids, or head to the gym for a bit. Watch other drinkers. Are they happy and chatty before they've had a drink? Of course not. They need a drink to get there, and even then they are lethargic and sedentary. See the alcoholic drinks for what they are; lots of refined sugar (which is itself a poison) mixed with a drug. When you see other drinkers sat there with their drinks imagine their hearts hammering away in their chests in direct response to the drug they've taken and how this makes them feel heavy and exhausted. Think of that anxious, insecure feeling that is slowly building up as their brain desperately tries to counter the depressive effects of the alcohol. Never take your sobriety for granted. It's all too easy to quit drinking and, because the benefits of sobriety come back over a few days or weeks and because you have them all the time, you take them as the norm and forget how drinking robbed you of them. The feeling of sobriety is the feeling of not being exhausted, of not being irritable, of not being anxious and lethargic. All of these things very soon become your norm. Never, ever, take them for granted, and think about them every time you see someone drinking. And I'm not just talking about problem drinkers or heavy drinkers. Every drinker who ever lived sacrificed far more to the false idol that is alcohol than they ever got in return.

Some people say we shouldn't criticise drinkers, that we are the ones with the problem, not them. They think that drinkers should be left to enjoy themselves and not miss out because of our issues. Let me be quite clear here, I would never ever say any of these things to a drinker (unless of course I was assisting them in becoming free). This is just how I perceive them. It is the reality of drinking as I see it and it is this perspective that has given me my freedom. I had two goals when writing these books. One was to tell the truth about alcohol as I see it. The second was to provide some tools to people to enable them to retake control of their lives from alcohol. It was never my intention to tell half-truths and lies to enable people to continue taking a drug. When I look at drinkers this is what I see and frankly it seems to me to be a far more accurate picture than that portrayed by society generally and by the drinkers themselves.

Freedom is reliant on seeing alcohol as it really is and seeing drinkers as they really are is part and parcel of that. If you are uncomfortable then as ever it is your prerogative to disregard what I am saying, but you do need to think about what your goal is. Is it to see the truth and regain control of your life? Or to continue to buy into the nonsense that caused you so many problems in the first place?

Going back to holidays though I also have children. For me being on holiday gives me an opportunity to spend some time with them. Children require patience and energy, two things alcohol robs you of. Remember the lady who emailed me to say that what was worrying her was that usually on holiday she'd start drinking around 3pm and from then until dinner was also her 'silly time' with the kids, a time she would play with them and mess around being silly with them? It wasn't until I read this that I realised I was doing what I say not to do a few paragraphs up, which is to never take for granted what your sobriety has given you. Until she sent me that email I didn't realise that even though I don't drink on holiday I still have silly time with my two boys. But mine isn't 3pm until dinner time, it runs approximately from the very second we all wake up and runs until the time we all collapse into bed (except perhaps for half an hour or so after lunch).

I have now been on holiday numerous times not drinking. I know every time that I go that it would be the easiest thing in the world to go to the bar and order a couple of drinks. But I know that even though the withdrawal from two drinks would be minor it would be there. It would be an unpleasant, anxious feeling and suddenly I wouldn't be enjoying the holiday, or enjoying playing with my sons, or enjoying my book or enjoying going for a walk, all I'd be thinking about was when I could have that next drink so I could get rid of that unpleasant feeling so I could then get on with enjoying my holiday. I wouldn't be enjoying myself because the usual stresses and strains of everyday life that are still there even when on holiday would suddenly be worrying me more and more and my ability to enjoy the holiday would drop away. I'd be having to keep drinking just to maintain the level of mental resilience I have all the time now that I'm not drinking. That would lead to lack of sleep, anxiousness and lethargy. And that of course is the third stage of our three-stage approach; how alcohol actually removes the genuine pleasure from the event.

Holidays are different when you aren't drinking and they are far better. They are a mix of quality sleep, reading, eating, chatting, charging around, seeing things, playing around and relaxing. This is opposed to when you are drinking when holidays are all about, well, drinking. About sitting around relieving the withdrawal. And of course going home feeling more wiped out than when you went.

Another event that causes people concern when they stop drinking is Christmas. Again let me tell you how I saw Christmas when I was drinking, and how I see it now.

My view of Christmas when I was drinking was the 'mistletoe and wine' Christmas. Mulled wine, log fires, time with friends and family, a Christmas meal with red wine, champagne for breakfast, and when the day was over cuddling up on the sofa with a mulled wine heavily laced with brandy.

The reality of course was very different. Lying awake for large chunks of the night before is never the best start to any day. The first few drinks were always a pleasure (but only because they were dulling the tiredness and remedying the chemical imbalance caused by the previous drinks), but after a few hours drinking, and a huge meal, the rest of the day would be spent asleep. Arguments were fairly common place, as they are I think for many people over Christmas.

I always loved Christmas as a child, it was such a magical and wonderful time of year. As I got older it became a drinking day, a day where you could drink as I liked so I loved it for that reason. When I stopped drinking I found a third way to love Christmas.

Christmas is a day off work, it's a day when you can either stay in all day with the family, or go to someone else's house and enjoy their hospitality. You have lots of nice food, time with friends and family, a few presents, and maybe even a film. What's not to like?

Remember that every single alcoholic drink that is drunk over Christmas will result in disturbed sleep, a corresponding feeling of anxiety, and the poisoning of a human body. And these are the effects experienced by the people having just one drink (and there are precious few of those). As the number of drinks an individual drinks on each occasion increases so do the ill effects, moving from disturbed sleep into full blown insomnia and the resulting exhaustion and lethargy over the following days, moving from anxiety into increasing worry and fear and eventually into full blown depression, and from almost imperceptible poisoning into full blown hangover, nausea, and headaches. And of course other effects then come into play, as our emotional wiring short circuits we end up with the arguments, tears, anger and, for many, physical violence. Money being spent that many cannot really afford. Health being eroded and seriously damaged.

Every child hit, or shouted at, or reduced to tears because their parents were either drunk or hungover, every argument that took place that wouldn't otherwise have taken place and has been caused by tiredness and anxiety that exists only because of the previous drinking, every drunken fight, every drunken arrest. Every drunken argument that kicks off, all the domestic violence. Every person who unwittingly drinks too much and loses every shred of dignity.

The reason I love Christmas now is because it is a time to spend with my family, to see my children enjoy the magic that I used to enjoy when I was their age. To know I am passing on a little of the wonder and true magic that is still left in the world to my children. It's a time to spend time in the warmth with friends, a time to be as free from arguments and anger and tears as it is possible to get with a young family. A time to be as happy as it is possible to be, bearing mind the usual stresses and worries of everyday life. A time for nice food and warmth and company. This is as close to the idea of the utopian Christmas as it is possible to get and it won't be because of alcohol that I experience it, in fact it will only be possible because alcohol no longer factors in my life; if it did then this wouldn't be what I could expect from Christmas, what I would be looking forward to would be more tiredness, arguments, hangovers and anxiety.

Another occasion for people is shows, concerts or sporting events. So the ideal is sitting there with a drink really enjoying the event. So how is that false? Well the event organisers never want people intoxicated, it causes no end of problems for them. One of the main ways they discourage heavy drinking is to slow the flow of drinks by cutting back on bar staff (which also saves them money). I have been to many shows, concerts and sporting events drinking. Invariably I miss half of it because I am queuing at the bar or trying to get to the toilet. The part of the show I do see I'm usually not paying attention to because I'm either thinking about how I'll get my next drink or waiting for the break in considerable discomfort because I need the toilet. The event is either spent wanting to have a drink or, if you can get a steady enough supply, forgetting most of what you are watching in any event. The pleasure in the occasion that alcohol robs you of is actually enjoying the actual event at all!

I hope I have managed to show you how to approach these definitive drinking occasions and how you need to start seeing them differently. Remember that it is a three-stage process. Firstly recognising that what you are imagining is in some significant ways false. Secondly identify the pleasure in the occasion that is there even if there is no alcohol. Thirdly, think of the pleasure that alcohol would actually remove from the occasion.

## 21. The Tools for Quitting - The Bad Days

Most people can understand how drinking upsets the delicate chemical balance in their brain, leaving them feeling anxious, out of sorts, and even out and out depressed. They therefore have a reasonable expectation when they stop drinking that they will be happier. This is indeed the case the majority of the time. The good times are better and more frequent, and the bad times are fewer and aren't so bad. Things that caused the drinker significant concern when they were drinking suddenly no longer seem quite so overwhelming.

However everyone has bad days, either caused by something specific or just by the mood changes that all human beings are susceptible to on occasion. You need to accept that you will have bad times even when you've stopped drinking. I've had a few emails from people saying they've stopped for X number of months but suddenly have a period when they felt low for a few days for no apparent reason, and do I think that this is some kind of delayed withdrawal, and is there a way to cure it? My answer is that I don't think it is delayed withdrawal, I think it is life, and the only cure for life that I know of is death. Remember, when you quit drinking life does get better, but it is still life, and life has bad times as well as good. Moreover in addition to this there is a very specific mental trap you need to be aware of.

Take a standard situation. You have a bad day at work, or you have an argument with your partner, or you have a bill you can't pay. Whatever the reason, you are miserable. If you haven't quit drinking at this point the 'solution' is obvious; take a drink. Of course drinking isn't a 'solution' at all in any accepted sense of the word. It won't start repairing the damaged relationship, it won't create a budget or extra income that might deal with the bill, and plan a solution to your problem at work. All it will do is anesthetise the worry for some small period of time, but for drinkers it's often the only 'solution' that they turn to.

The problem is of course when the same thing happens when you've quit drinking. You have the argument or get the bill or have a bad day at work and your first thought is to take a drink because that is how your brain has been conditioned to respond for however many years or decades you have been drinking for.

So you start thinking about drinking. You start to think that a drink will relieve your misery. Of course it won't, it will just add to it considerably firstly by the sense of failure because you once again failed to stop drinking, and secondly because the physiological relief is so short lived and is then replaced by a corresponding feeling of anxiety. However assuming you don't take that drink you are miserable, only now you aren't miserable and thinking about the argument / bill / work whatever, now (in your mind at least) you are miserable because you can't drink. Because you believe that drink will provide a 'solution' you start to blame the misery not on the argument / bill / work, but on the fact that you've stopped drinking.

Very soon our mindset changes from the correct position, which is 'I am miserable because of work / finances / relationship issues' to 'I am miserable because I can't drink'.

Just as drinking gets the credit for benefits that it doesn't cause (such as the dopamine rush we get when we are socialising) so 'not drinking' often gets the blame for any misery which is in fact caused by issues completely unrelated to the fact that we have stopped drinking.

When you stop drinking you need to accept that it's not a ticket to paradise. It will result in a startlingly better quality of life but there will still be bad times albeit they will be far fewer and far less overwhelming than when you were drinking. There can be many reasons for these bad times, many possible causes, but your stopping drinking will not be one of them. Don't fall into the trap of blaming your unhappiness on the fact that you have stopped drinking.

The second point here is one I have mentioned previously, and that is to ensure that you have a plan in place for when the bad times hit (as they invariably will). Exercise, read, watch a film, get a punch bag and pummel it, meditate, do some yoga, have a nice meal, go to sleep, whatever but make sure you have it ready to go for when it's needed. Because it will be needed.

## 22. The Tools for Quitting - Religion

AA introduced the idea of a spiritual approach to quitting drinking so when people try AA and find for whatever reason that it is not right for them, there is a tendency to disregard the spiritual side of things entirely when looking at other methods of quitting. This is fine if you are not a spiritual person anyway but if you are then the spiritual side of things can be a powerful tool in your quitting.

When examining this topic it's worth remembering that alcohol anaesthetises. This means that when we are drinking we tend to be able to ignore problems in our life that we would otherwise find intolerable and that (without the alcohol) we would take steps to rectify. It ranges from little things like not bothering to shave, or tidy up, or make proper meals, to much bigger things like ignoring bills, not bothering to work at a relationship, or even staying in an otherwise toxic relationship. It is a self-propelling problem. When we are drunk or hungover we just don't feel mentally equipped to deal with things but those things don't go away, they stay there in the back of our mind like a cloud forever hanging over us, making us all the more likely to reach for a drink to take the edge off our ever increasing worries which leaves us even more drunk and / or hungover. And so the cycle continues.

So when people stop drinking they often face a swathe of problems that they need to do something about now that they can no longer hide from them behind a haze of alcohol. The good news is that as the person returns to their usual level of mental resilience and confidence they feel far better equipped to deal with these problems, even those that may have seemed insurmountable when they were drinking. These problems could be relationship problems, work problems, financial problems, losing weight, eating better, taking exercise, etc. If the person is ordinarily spiritual there may well be a spiritual element to this. People who are religious may well neglect their religious beliefs and practices when they are drinking causing them to feel guilt and conflict and find when they stop they naturally look to rectify this.

It's also the case as I have mentioned several times that quitting drinking isn't just about not taking another drink, it is about finding something else to turn to when times get hard. Religious or spiritual beliefs can be exactly the tool to use when times get hard. It can help people to put up with adversity, to face their own mortality, and to make sense of their time on this planet.

I think that it is worth bearing in mind for everyone, spiritual and non-spiritual alike, that religious and spiritual beliefs are incredibly complicated, and belief is not something you can simply choose. Trying to convince yourself that you believe in something when you don't believe in it creates a false foundation. Whatever you then build on that foundation is a tower just waiting to collapse. It is a frustrating and ultimately pointless process. For many, convincing them that their sobriety is reliant on believing in something that they cannot believe in is akin to telling them that they can never quit. It is a death sentence, or in many ways worse than a death sentence, because the misery caused by long term heavy drinking is often worse than death (which the suicide rates among those with alcohol dependency is a stark testament to).

The reverse is absolutely the case too. Some people are spiritual. When they stop drinking they will turn again to the spiritual side of their lives, and they will use that as the coping mechanism where once they relied on alcohol. Denying them a spiritual solution is just as much a death sentence for them as forcing the spiritual solution on someone who does not have it in their nature to believe that the solution to their problem is religious or spiritual.

If you are in any way spiritual or religious then you should try to cultivate this when you stop drinking as it can be another powerful tool in your new life.

## 23. The Tools for Quitting – A Positive Approach

I am a fairly pragmatic and practical person and on the whole I find people telling me to believe in myself and to 'visualise yourself succeeding' irritating. I particularly dislike the notion that visualising success will ensure you obtain it. I have no doubt it works for some people, but some people succeed anyway. If ten athletes are running a race no doubt they all visualise winning. Then when the winner is interviewed we hear how they visualised winning and assume this assisted them. It's a shame we never hear from the 9 who didn't win about how well their positive thinking worked for them. I remember reading that Jim Carrey visualised himself getting paid $10m for acting and this was what he ended up getting paid for Dumb and Dumber. Amazing. I wonder how many of the vast majority of other actors who never actually made it to the bigtime used a similar technique to no avail. Unfortunately we will never hear from them as it's only those who succeeded who we ever hear from.

Positive thinking cannot make things happen but it can (if used correctly) keep us in a more positive state of mind and this can have a profound impact on overcoming addiction. Let me give you an example.

Let's say you are going out to a big social function and you are resolved not to drink at it. Let's see how your state of mind (which you can control) can affect the outcome.

Firstly let's say that you are scared and nervous and worrying about it because you aren't going to drink. You are worried about how you'll cope, what people will think of you, you know you're not going to enjoy yourself without drinking so the whole thing is going to be a chore. You turn up, you feel increasingly nervous and loathe to attend. When there you spend your time obsessing about (not) drinking. You don't really engage in conversation because that requires a degree of relaxation and effort which you can't muster. Other people of course will pick up on this and will find you hard work, so you are far more likely to find yourself alone which makes you feel even more self-conscious and miserable, after all everyone else seems to be chatting away and enjoying themselves, it's only you who are standing alone feeling utterly miserable. You are different to everyone else. They can all enjoy themselves and relax and have a good time. You've given up the only thing you really enjoyed about going out so you're not going to enjoy socialising anymore. You have to stand there, as alone as if you didn't have another human within a thousand square miles of you, watching everyone else engage and have fun. But you aren't going to drink so you grit your teeth and suffer the evening. You are an alcoholic, one of the tainted few, this evening is about hard and unpleasant work. You are working your recovery, it's important and you will do it but let's not pretend you are going to enjoy it. Your chances of getting a 'feel good' boost are zero.

This time let's say you take a slightly different mental approach to the evening. First off you aren't going to drink. That's a given. Come hell or high water, good times or bad, you won't drink. Worst case you will walk out and leave if you have to but whatever happens you won't drink so you don't even need to worry about that. Given that as your starting point you are going to go along and enjoy yourself as best you can. Everyone else will be drinking but so what? They are idiots and doing what they do out of ignorance. They are still mired in the lies and hype and they pay dearly for their ignorance, but that's their lookout, it's nothing you're going to worry about. In fact it plays into your favour, after all you probably will feel a bit self-conscious (who doesn't at social occasions?) and at least you know that after the first hour or so when the drink starts to take them over they will be incapable of noticing you or caring about you or remembering what you did and said anyway. Their intoxication provides you protection against being noticed, it allows you to walk unseen among them. You may even try the dreaded sober dancing, after all why not? No one else will notice you and you won't look any more stupid than when you danced drunk. If you're going to do a sober night out you may as well really go for it. After all, what's the worst that can happen? If you make a complete fool of yourself and people do notice they'll just assume you're drunk! You are going to go, chat or not chat, dance or not dance, stay late or leave. You will do whatever you like to enjoy yourself. If you get a 'feel good' serotonin / endorphin boost so much the better, if you don't so what? If you do get one at least you'll be able to enjoy it as opposed to anaesthetising it and replacing it with numbness. After all that's what the drinkers do. The drinking may allow them to access slightly quicker that feel good boost but the subsequent drinks then anaesthetise it. You'll eat when you want to eat, you'll have a soft drink when you want to drink, and you'll leave and go home when you've had enough. There won't be any chemical inside you forcing you to drink more even though your body doesn't need any more liquid, eat even though you're not hungry, and stay out even when it's way past time you went home. You'll sleep well and wake up feeling as bright and raring to go as you ever do. So even if the evening is rubbish for any reason it won't ruin the following day as well. You are going to forget all the nonsense about being 'in recovery', about the stereotypes about 'alcoholics trying to quit' who are miserable and depressed and bitter, about nights out not being as much fun without a drink. You are going to keep things in perspective, which are that you were addicted to a drug and it made you miserable but now you've quit and you can live the best life you can and it starts tonight. You'll go out, have whatever fun you can, and then leave. What you aren't going to do is bemoan the fact that you aren't still dwelling in ignorance and denial like everyone who is still drinking. And at the end of the evening, even if it was the worst night in the entire history of the human race, you will be going home sober and will have proved to yourself and others that you can go out for an evening without drinking.

Which of these two approaches do you think are going to give you the most enjoyable evening?

Which of these approaches do you think is going to end up with you leaving at the end of the evening thinking 'I can't believe it I cracked it, I went out and had a great night not drinking!'?

Which of these approaches is going to be a major stopping stone in your new sober life?

Above all, which of these approaches is going to mean you face your next sober social event with ten times more confidence and motivation?

In the same way you need to see through the lies and hype that cover the ugly truth about drinking, so you also need to see through the hype and ugly lies that cover the beautiful truth about sobriety. Sobriety isn't (or at least it needn't be) about moping around, taking one day at a time, resisting temptation and living a half-life at best. It shouldn't be about envying 'normal' drinkers and wishing you could be like them. It shouldn't be about being in recovery and working every day to stay sober. It should be a celebration, it should be about enthusiastically embracing a new and far better life, it should be about looking at drinkers with pity (after all they give up so much for so little return and they do it through ignorance and not through genuine choice).

Drinkers, at whatever stage they are at, are taking a poison that accelerates their heart rate which makes them lethargic, they are spoiling their sleep, they are taking on extra calories they don't need and overeating which itself makes them uncomfortable and additionally lethargic. They suffer anxiety when the drink wears off and they have to pay good money for this substance. And this is the light drinkers. The more people drink the more all of these problems are exacerbated and the more they wish they could stop but at the same time the more they believe that they can't truly enjoy life without drinking. What on earth is there to envy? Why should you who have stopped drinking be moping around miserable? You should be jumping for joy! It's the poor drinkers who should be moping around miserable (and they are most of the time anyway).

When you look at other drinkers see the truth about what they are doing. See it without the hype. See the highly sugared poison for what it is. Think about how their heart and brain is labouring to counter the poisonous depressive effects of the poison. Think of the feeling of lethargy it causes. See that the joy they get from drinking is in no small part just dampening the anxiety caused by their previous drinks. See how short lived the 'pleasure' is, how the intoxication soon takes over and how they become dulled instead of jolly. Think about how they will be tossing and turning all night, lying awake anxious and afraid, to finally get up exhausted, anxious and irritable to spend a day feeling miserable and anxious and lethargic (unless of course they dampen all the negative feelings with yet more doses of the same poison).

The bottom line is that taking a positive approach is a hugely powerful technique. Remember that what you are doing is a fantastic thing; you are solving a problem and moving on to a far better life. There is no reason to feel intimidated and timid.

## 24. Conclusion

As covered at the very start of this book, addiction, any addiction, is where the addict believes that they need their drug of choice to fully enjoy and cope with life. Whilst they retain this belief they will keep returning to their drug. So to successfully quit a drug you need to change your core beliefs about it.

On the one hand this makes alcohol one of the most difficult drugs to quit because it is alcohol, over and above any other drug, where we are bombarded daily with misinformation about it. This ranges from the obvious forms like adverts for alcoholic drinks (which show us that alcohol is social, fun and relaxing) to our friends, family, colleagues, and even complete strangers all telling us, and posting images telling us, (overtly and subtly) that alcohol relaxes us, helps us have a good time, is good for us, is sociable, and that life will never quite be the same without it. The reason for this is primarily historical and is due to the ease with which alcohol can be created. Many other drugs require delicate chemical processes to make them or require ingredients that are difficult to manufacture or cultivate. This is not the case with alcohol where you just need some rotting fruit or vegetable matter. Because it is so easy to create its consumption has become widespread and in this way normalised. Because we have taken this drug for so many generations it has become very closely intertwined with our culture to such an extent that to be addicted to it is the norm and to reject it is seen as not only unusual but often strange and antisocial.

In this way quitting alcohol is more difficult to quit than any other drug, but what is in our favour is how little alcohol gives to us compared to what it takes. If you had never experienced any drugs of any kind before in your life and I gave you a selection of 50 different drugs and asked you to rate them in order of how good they made you feel, alcohol would be way down in the list. There are drugs out there that make you feel genuinely euphoric, truly alive and happy and all but bursting with joy. These drugs have side effects even more immediately devastating than alcohol but assume you are only rating them on their immediate effect. Alcohol just makes you feel slightly dulled. It's only because of the occasion that we tend to take it on (it can speed up a natural serotonin / endorphin high when you are socialising) and because it is chemically addictive (i.e. it makes you feel insecure and unhappy and then relieves that feeling) that we believe it does far more for us than it actually does. In this way alcohol starts to become a far easier addiction to tackle.

To successfully quit drinking you need to see drinking in a whole new way. You need to see drinkers in a whole new way. You need to see recovery in a whole new way and yourself in a whole new way. Finally you need to see those situations that you believe you will never be able to enjoy without alcohol in a whole new way. You need to see the truth and not the facade of it all. You need to see the truth behind the images and hype that you are constantly bombarded with. The vast majority of people in Western society drink and unfortunately they feel insecure about their drinking at a fairly deep level and so have a vested interest in perpetuating the 'sweetness and light' lie that covers the ugly truth about drinking. That's all very well for them but it makes it hard for those of us who wish to see the truth and not the illusion, who wish to live the best life we can instead of blindly following the other lemmings over the cliff edge.

What I have tried to do in this book and Alcohol Explained is to use a bit of common sense and clear thought to fully analyse alcohol so we can see it for what it really is. With this in mind I think it is useful to summarise below the main points we've covered off:

1. Alcohol is a chemical depressant and when you drink it your brain takes various steps to counter the depressive effects of the alcohol. When the alcohol then wears off you are left feeling overly anxious and nervous.

2. Never underestimate the extent to which alcohol drags you down, or how much sobriety lifts you up. Because these states are constant we tend to take them both for granted. When we are drinking we tend not to realise how below par we are, let alone do we blame that on

our drinking. When we stop we quickly take our improved state for granted and soon forget how much alcohol really dragged us down.

3. If you do take a drink after you are through the physical withdrawal it will do even less for you than it did during your drinking days. There will be a dulled feeling but no 'boost' (the boost is just relieving the withdrawal so in this way, when you quit, you are already living the boost 24 hours a day). It will however, make you feel miserable as you will have failed to quit.

4. It is only ever the idea and not the reality of drinking that pulls us back. The reality never measures up to the idea. Remember that over time your perception of alcohol and drinking will slowly warp, like wood that is allowed to become damp. Imagine you have a house that is warm and safe with a wooden door. Over time, if you don't maintain it, that wooden door will slowly warp and will start letting in the cold wind and rain. Your security will have been compromised. Watch out for that. When you notice the rot setting in it is time to do some remedial work. You do this by sticking close to reality which will prevent you from starting to believe the hype and lies.

5. There is no 'buzz' to drinking. The buzz is either the relieving of the previous withdrawal, tiredness and lethargy, or hastening (and then dulling) a natural serotonin / endorphin high.

6. Think about those occasions that you thought could only ever be enjoyable with a drink. Use the three-pronged approach in advance of attending them:

   a) Recognise how the drinking utopia you imagine is false.
   b) Identify the true pleasure in the occasion that stands independently of any alcohol.
   c) Recognise how alcohol actually detracts from instead of enhances the event.

7. If you identify a difficult situation coming up then identify the tipping point and run through in your mind how you will deal with it.

8. See drinkers as they really are. When you see them drinking imagine the cancerous poisons thinly veiled with mounds of refined sugar. Think of the dulled feeling as the alcohol kicks in, how it anesthetises not only any anxiety but also any true serotonin /endorphin high. Imagine that horrible anxious feeling building up as the drink wears off and how they will need another drink to relieve it. Think about how it will make them overeat and how their heart will be speeding up as their body and brain reacts to the poison, how this in turn will make them feel heavy and lethargic. Imagine them tossing and turning all night, robbed of the restorative sleep that they

so badly need. If they are drinking too much see how their eyes dull and glaze over, how their personality dulls as they repeat themselves, standing too close to you, and thinking that they are considerably more entertaining than they are.

9. See yourself as you really are. Someone who had the strength of character to identify a problem and actually do something about it, instead of pathetically pretending there is nothing to worry about when there so clearly is. Nearly 90% of the population need a drug to enjoy themselves. You don't anymore. That takes imagination, strength of character and independence. This is your new self-image; the self-image of a non-drinker.

10. When you stop know that it is for good. Many people find quitting easy when the groundwork is properly laid, others find that it is still hard work. For most people it fluctuates between the two, and can get progressively easier as the reality of sobriety starts to hit home. A good way of approaching it is to hope for the best but prepare for the worst. Expect is to be hard work and a struggle, expect to have to dig deep to stick with it. Then if it is hard work you are prepared and if it isn't (or when you hit those times when you start to enjoy it and feel like you can really do it) then this is a bonus. If you have properly changed your view of alcohol you should find stopping far more manageable and even enjoyable but don't worry too much if you are still riddled with doubts. The best thing to do is to stop

happily and confidently. The second-best thing to do is to stop but be riddled with doubts and find it hard and unpleasant work. The worst thing to do is to keep drinking. Make a commitment to stop and know that whether it is hard or easy you are better off than if you were to continue drinking. Just commit to stopping and know that it is for the best whatever happens. Remember that no one can force you to take another drink.

11. See 'recovery' for what it is. It is you stopping taking a poison and the only reason you have been taking it for so long is that your brain's automated survival mechanisms have been tricked by the effects of the drug. Your life improves immeasurably the minute you stop taking it.

12. When you do stop you can expect a few unpleasant days while your body and brain gets back to normal. The process for this is as follows (full details of this can be found in chapter 4):

a) The alcohol needs to leave your system.

b) The excess stimulation needs to abate. During this period you will feel tense, anxious, possibly shaky. You will find you can eat less and may struggle sleeping.

c) Regular drinkers will then face a period where their brain gets used to the lack of excess stimulation that has been ever present for however long the drinker has been drinking for. This is a period of feeling tired, dazed and sleeping lots.

d) After these stages you then need to get back to a normal sleeping pattern and catch up on lost sleep.

13. Go out and enjoy your new sober life. Quitting drinking is about living your life without a drink, not hiding from it. Don't be afraid to go straight out into daunting situations. As long as you are properly prepared you will be fine. Some people decide that they want to get through the above withdrawal process first, others decide they want to get stuck into their new life as soon as possible. Do what is right for you but tackling difficult situations without drinking is what defines success.

14. If you genuinely feel like you can't go through certain situations without drinking then it is your prerogative to avoid them, but remember that if you do feel this way it is more likely that changing your mindset, rather than time, that will provide the solution.

15. Often when people quit drinking they feel under par for a few days as they go through the above process but then one day they wake up to feel extraordinarily different. They feel rested, alive, positive,

happy and resilient in a way that they haven't felt in years. It's a whole world from waking up groggy and anxious and hungover. It's an even better feeling than those first crucial drinks at one of your definitive drinking experiences. This feeling is the feeling of being alive, of living a life where the delicate chemical balance of your brain is not in disarray. It is how human beings are supposed to feel. It is the great pleasure of not drinking. Just be wary though as it is a feeling that you very quickly get used to and start to take for granted. It is also a feeling that alcohol cannot improve upon. If you take a drink now there is no withdrawal, no sleep deprivation, no lethargy to anaesthetise. When you get to this stage know that all a drink will do is dull that wonderful feeling.

16. If you don't wake up one day experiencing this don't worry. Not everyone goes through this. Some people may be sleeping badly for completely unrelated reasons. Others may have genuine problems that they need to deal with which take the shine off things. Be aware that just because you don't experience this feeling as a really noticeable event doesn't mean you aren't getting there. For some people that return to the wonderful feeling of being normal is a more gradual process and so not necessarily so obvious.

17. With sleep remember there are a few things you can do to assist (full details of this can be found in chapter 2):

a)  Avoid caffeine particularly later in the day.

b)  Try to do as much exercise / physical activity as you can, and as early in the day as you can manage.

c)  Avoid eating large meals later in the day.

d)  If you are waking up regularly in the night think about going to bed a bit later and try to stick to a regular waking up time.

e)  When you go to bed don't think about all the stresses and strains of life but concentrate on something relaxing and peaceful.

18. Have a plan in place to deal with the bad times because they will come. Plan how you will deal with them. Run, walk, read, meet friends, watch a film, go to bed, do some yoga, meditate, or rediscover religion. Whatever it is have it ready for when you need it.

19. Whatever plan you have in place to deal with stress do try to do some exercise. Many people find the idea of exercising repugnant and view people who exercise regularly as freaks who are obsessed with how they look and living for as long as they can. In fact people exercise for the simple reason that it makes them feel good; exercise releases serotonin and endorphins and helps you sleep better. Mostly people only find exercise abhorrent because the drugs they

take accelerate their heart rate which makes exercising difficult and uncomfortable. Humans aren't designed to be sedentary. They are designed to move.

20. If you are ever triggered to drink because of negative emotions remember that alcohol will increase these substantially.

21. Moderation is not an option. It never was and it never will be.

22. If you haven't already stopped drinking set a date to do so and until that day really concentrate on the whole experience of drinking and think constantly how different you would be feeling if you weren't drinking (see chapter 14). When you do finally come to stop it might be worth rereading Chapter 14.

23. Stopping drinking provides the key to weightloss, it doesn't guarantee it.

24. Don't forget what cravings are; they are you fantasising about how nice it would be to take a drink. There are two ways to defeat them, certainty and reality.

25. Keep positive about quitting. You are giving up some very unpleasant experiences and making phenomenal gains. You are

never going to drink again come what may, nothing can change that, so you may as well make the best of whatever the future holds.

I hope you have found this book to be useful and interesting. If you have then I would ask two things of you. Firstly please take the time to leave a review on Amazon. Secondly please recommend it to others. To be a successful author these days you need two things; a good book and a successful marketing strategy. Whatever strengths I may possess, marketing and self-promotion is not one of them. My marketing strategy is therefore very simple; I cross my fingers and hope that you, the reader, will recommend this book to others.

If you are interested in making contact with me then you can do so through the website (www.alcoholexplained.com). I also have an Instagram account (alcoholexplained). Alternatively please do join me in the Alcohol Explained Facebook Group. I hope to see you there.

Printed in Great Britain
by Amazon